Lonely Planet

P9-CEY-990

Pocket
ROME
TOP SIGHTS • LOCAL LIFE • MADE EASY

Duncan Garwood, Nicola Williams

In This Book

QuickStart Guide

Your keys to understanding the city – we help you decide what to do and how to do it

Need to Know
Tips for a smooth trip

Neighbourhoods
What's where

Explore Rome

The best things to see and do, neighbourhood by neighbourhood

Top Sights
Make the most of your visit

Local Life
The insider's city

The Best of Rome

The city's highlights in handy lists to help you plan

Best Walks
See the city on foot

Rome's Best...
The best experiences

Survival Guide

Tips and tricks for a seamless, hassle-free city experience

Getting Around
Travel like a local

Essential Information
Including where to stay

Our selection of the city's best places to eat, drink and experience:

◎ **Sights**

✖ **Eating**

🍷 **Drinking**

✿ **Entertainment**

🛍 **Shopping**

These symbols give you the vital information for each listing:

🕿 Telephone Numbers	🖼 Family-Friendly
⊙ Opening Hours	🐾 Pet-Friendly
P Parking	🚌 Bus
Ⓝ Nonsmoking	⛴ Ferry
@ Internet Access	Ⓜ Metro
🛜 Wi-Fi Access	Ⓢ Subway
🥗 Vegetarian Selection	🚋 Tram
🍴 English-Language Menu	🚆 Train

Find each listing quickly on maps for each neighbourhood:

Bar Hemingway

16 🍷 Map p233, B2

Legend has it that Hemi
self, wielding a machine
...rate this timber-pan
...ered bar during
...showpiece is a
...en by Papa ar
... town. Dress
...s.com; Hôtel Rit
...; ⊙6.30pm-2a

Lonely Planet's Rome

Lonely Planet Pocket Guides are designed to get you straight to the heart of the city.

Inside you'll find all the must-see sights, plus tips to make your visit to each one really memorable. We've split the city into easy-to-navigate neighbourhoods and provided clear maps so you'll find your way around with ease. Our expert writers have searched out the best of the city: walks, food, nightlife and shopping, to name a few. Because you want to explore, our 'Local Life' pages will take you to some of the most exciting areas to experience the real Rome.

And of course you'll find all the practical tips you need for a smooth trip: itineraries for short visits, how to get around, and how much to tip the guy who serves you a drink at the end of a long day's exploration.

It's your guarantee of a really great experience.

Our Promise

You can trust our travel information because Lonely Planet writers visit the places we write about, each and every edition. We never accept freebies for positive coverage, so you can rely on us to tell it like it is.

QuickStart Guide 7

Explore Rome 21

Worth a Trip:

The Best of Rome 151

Rome's Best Walks

Rome's Best...

Survival Guide 173

QuickStart Guide

Welcome to Rome

A heady mix of haunting ruins, awe-inspiring art and vibrant street life, Italy's hot-blooded capital is one of the world's most romantic and enticing cities. A trip to Rome is as much about lapping up the *dolce vita* lifestyle as gorging on art and culture, while the city's ancient icons recall its golden age as *caput mundi* (capital of the world). Visit once and you'll be hooked for life.

Fontana dei Quattro Fiumi (p44), Piazza Navona
BELENOS/SHUTTERSTOCK ©

Rome
Top Sights

Colosseum (p24)
Rome's awe-inspiring
ancient amphitheatre.

Villa Borghese
(p146)
Sensational sculptures
and Renaissance
masterpieces.

Pantheon (p38)
triumph of ancient architecture.

Vatican Museums (p132)
Sistine Chapel and jaw-dropping art.

St Peter's Basilica (p136)

The Vatican's majestic showpiece church.

Appian Way (p92)

One of the world's oldest roads.

Roman Forum (p26)

Ancient Rome's nerve centre.

Trevi Fountain (p68)
Rome's most famous fountain.

Basilica di San Giovanni in Laterano (p98)
Monumental papal basilica.

VVOE/SHUTTERSTOCK ©

Spanish Steps & Piazza di Spagna (p56)
People-watching on Rome's celebrated steps.

Rome
Local Life

*Local experiences and hidden gem
to help you uncover the real cit*

It's easy to be blinded by Rome's beauty, but scratch beneath the surface and you'll discover another side to the city. Here we explore the city's alternative hang-outs an boho bars, its hot clubs and off-the-radar neighbourhoods.

A Day Out in the Centro Storico (p40)
☑ Beautiful backdrops ☑ Shopping and craft beer

San Lorenzo & Pigneto (p78)
☑ Historic churches and cemeteries
☑ Chocolate and wine tastings

Ostiense & San Paolo (p106)
☑ Street art and ancient sculpture ☑ Cool clubs

Other great ways to experience the city like a local:

Night Out in Trastavere & Gianicolo (p120)
☑ Aperitivo ☑ Live music

Rome
Day Planner

Day One

Start the day at the **Colosseum** (p24), Rome's huge gladiatorial arena – try to get there early to avoid the queues. Then head down to the **Palatino** (p31) to poke around crumbling ruins and admire sweeping views. From the Palatino, follow on to the **Roman Forum** (p26), an evocative area of tumbledown temples, sprouting columns and ruined basilicas.

After lunch climb up to **Piazza del Campidoglio** (p32) and the **Capitoline Museums** (p32), where you'll find some sensational ancient sculpture. Done there, enjoy great views from the **Vittoriano** (p33) before pushing on to the *centro storico* (historic centre) to explore its labyrinthine medieval streets and head-line sights such as the **Pantheon** (p38) and **Piazza Navona** (p44).

After dinner get a taste of dolce vita bar life. Depending on what you're after, you could hang out with the beautiful people at chic **Etablì** (p50) near Piazza Navona, chat over coffee at **Caffè Sant'Eustachio** (p49), or sup cocktails at the **Gin Corner** (p50).

Day Two

On day two, hit the Vatican. First up are the **Vatican Museums** (p132). Once you've blown your mind on the Sistine Chapel and its other myriad masterpieces, complete your tour at **St Peter's Basilica** (p136). If you have the energy, climb its Michelangelo-designed dome for fantastic views over **St Peter's Square** (p142).

Jump on the metro and head back over the river to check out **Piazza di Spagna** (p56). Plan your moves while sitting on the Spanish Steps, then push on to the **Trevi Fountain** (p68) where tradition dictates you throw a coin into the water to ensure your return to Rome. Next, head up the hill to catch the sunset on **Piazza del Quirinale** (p73) in front of the presidential palace, Palazzo del Quirinale.

Spend the evening in the buzzing area around **Campo de' Fiori** (p51). **Barnum Cafe** (p49) is a top place for cocktails and laid-back tunes or hit **Open Baladin** (p41) for a welcome taste of craft beer.

Short on time?

We've arranged Rome's must-sees into these day-by-day itineraries to make sure you see the very best of the city in the time you have available.

Day Three

On day three starts with a trip to the **Museo e Galleria Borghese** (p147) – don't forget to book – to marvel at amazing baroque sculpture. Afterwards, stroll through **Villa Borghese** (p147) down to **La Galleria Nazionale** (p148) for an injection of modern art.

In the afternoon, check what's going on at Rome's modernist cultural centre, the **Auditorium Parco della Musica** (p148), before heading back to **Piazza del Popolo** (p59). Just off the piazza, the **Basilica di Santa Maria del Popolo** (p59) is a magnificent repository of art. Next, dedicate some time to browsing the flagship stores and designer boutiques in the upscale streets off Via del Corso.

Over the river, the picture-perfect Trastevere neighbourhood bursts with life in the evening as locals and tourists flock to its many eateries and bars. Get into the mood with a glass of Tuscan red and regional snacks at **La Prosciutteria** (p125) before hitting the hard stuff at **Pimm's Good** (p126).

Day Four

On day four it's time to venture out to the **Appian Way** (p93). The main attractions here are the catacombs, and it's a wonderfully creepy sensation to duck down into these sinister pitch-black tunnels.

Once you've eaten, head north to Stazione Termini and the nearby **Museo Nazionale Romano: Palazzo Massimo alle Terme** (p82), a superb museum full of classical sculpture and stunning mosaics. Then, drop by the monumental **Basilica di Santa Maria Maggiore** (p85), famous for its mosaics, and the **Basilica di San Pietro in Vincoli** (p86), home to Michelangelo's muscular Moses sculpture. Finish up with some shopping in the fashionable boutiques of the charming Monti district.

Stay put in Monti, where there's plenty of late-night action. Take your pick of wine bar or cafe to see out the day. **La Bottega del Caffè** (p90) is an ever-popular hang-out.

Need to Know

For more information, see Survival Guide (p173)

Language
Italian

Visas
Not required by EU citizens. Not required by nationals of Australia, Canada, New Zealand and the USA for stays of up to 90 days.

Money
Currency is the € (euro). ATMs are widespread. Major credit cards are widely accepted but some smaller shops, trattorias and hotels might not take them.

Mobile Phones
Local SIM cards can be used in European, Australian and unlocked US phones. Other phones must be set to roaming.

Time
Italy is in a single time zone, one hour ahead of GMT. Daylight-saving time, when clocks move forward one hour, starts on the last Sunday in March. Clocks are put back an hour on the last Sunday in October. Italy operates on a 24-hour clock, so 6pm is written as 18:00.

Plugs & Adaptors
Plugs have two or three round pins; electricity is 220V to 230V. North American travellers will require an adaptor and transformer.

Tipping
Romans are not big tippers, but round up to the nearest euro in a taxi. Service (*servizio*) is generally included in the bill at restaurants.

① Before You Go

Your Daily Budget

Budget: Less than €110
▶ Dorm bed: €20–35
▶ Double room in a budget hotel: €60–130
▶ Pizza plus beer: €15

Midrange: €110–250
▶ Double room in a hotel: €110–200
▶ Local restaurant meal: €25–45
▶ Admission to museum: €5–16

Top end: More than €250
▶ Double room in a four- or five-star hotel: €200–450
▶ Top restaurant dinner: €45–150
▶ Opera ticket €17–150
▶ City-centre taxi ride €10–15

Useful Websites

▶ **Turismo Roma** (www.turismoroma.it) Rome's official tourist website.

▶ **060608** (www.060608.it) Sights, transport, upcoming events.

▶ **Lonely Planet** (www.lonelyplanet.com/rome) Destination information, hotel bookings, traveller forum and more.

Advance Planning

Two months before Book high-season accommodation.

One to two weeks before Book tables at A-list restaurants; tickets for the pope's weekly audience; and a visit to Palazzo Farnese.

Few days before Book tickets for the Museo e Galleria Borghese (compulsory) and for the Vatican Museums and Colosseum (advisable).

② Arriving in Rome

Most people arrive in Rome by plane, landing at one of its two airports: Leonardo da Vinci, better known as Fiumicino, or Ciampino, a hub for European low-cost carrier Ryanair. As an alternative to short-haul flights, trains serve Rome's main station, Stazione Termini, from a number of European destinations as well as cities across Italy.

✈ From Leonardo da Vinci (Fiumicino) Airport

• Leonardo Express trains to Stazione Termini 6.23am to 11.23pm, €14;

• slower FL1 trains to Trastevere, Ostiense and Tiburtina stations 5.57am to 10.42pm, €8;

• buses to Stazione Termini 6.05am to 12.30am, €6;

• private transfers from €22 per person;

• taxis €48 (fixed fare to within the Aurelian Walls).

✈ From Ciampino Airport

• Buses to Stazione Termini 4am to 11.15pm, €5;

• private transfers €25 per person;

• taxis €30 (fixed fare to within the Aurelian Walls).

🚌 From Stazione Termini

Airport buses and trains, and international trains, arrive at Stazione Termini. From here, continue by bus, metro or taxi.

③ Getting Around

Public transport includes buses, trams, metro and a suburban train network. The main hub is Stazione Termini. Tickets, which come in various forms, are valid for all types of transport. Children under 10 years travel free.

Ⓜ Metro

The metro is quicker than surface transport but the network is limited. There are two main lines, A (orange) and B (blue), which cross at Stazione Termini. Trains run between 5.30am and 11.30pm (to 1.30am on Fridays and Saturdays).

🚌 Buses

Most routes pass through Stazione Termini. Buses run approximately 5.30am until midnight, with limited services throughout the night.

🏃 On Foot

Rome is a sprawling city, but the historic centre is relatively compact. Distances are not great and walking is often the best way of getting around.

Rome Neighbourhoods

Tridente (p54)
Designer stores and swanky bars set the tone for this stylish, upmarket district centred on two striking piazzas.
⊙ Top Sights
Spanish Steps & Piazza di Spagna

Vatican City & Prati (p130)
Feast on extravagant art in the monumental Vatican and excellent food in neighbouring Prati.
⊙ Top Sights
Vatican Museums
St Peter's Basilica

Centro Storico (p36)
Rome's historic centre is the capital's thumping heart – a heady warren of famous squares and tangled lanes, galleries, restaurants and bars.
⊙ Top Sights
Pantheon

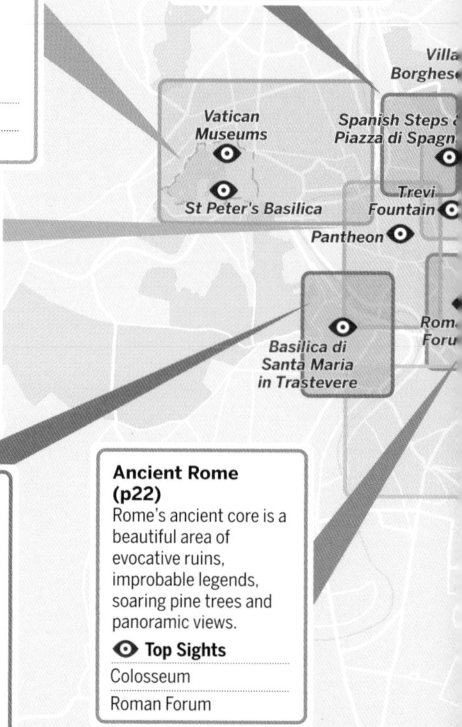

Trastevere & Gianicolo (p116)
Trastevere's medieval streets heave with kicking bars and eateries. The Gianicolo offers to-die-for panoramas.
⊙ Top Sights
Basilica di Santa Maria in Trastevere

Ancient Rome (p22)
Rome's ancient core is a beautiful area of evocative ruins, improbable legends, soaring pine trees and panoramic views.
⊙ Top Sights
Colosseum
Roman Forum

Villa Borghese

Vatican Museums ⊙

Spanish Steps & Piazza di Spagna

⊙ St Peter's Basilica

Trevi Fountain ⊙

Pantheon ⊙

Rome Forum

⊙ Basilica di Santa Maria in Trastevere

Trevi & the Quirinale (p66)

A busy, hilly district, home to Rome's most famous fountain, Italy's presidential palace and several stellar art galleries.

⊙ Top Sights

Trevi Fountain

Monti & Esquilino (p80)

Boutiques and wine bars abound in Monti, while Esquilino offers multiculturalism and several must-see museums and churches.

⊙ Top Sights

Museo Nazionale Romano: Palazzo Massimo alle Terme

⊙ *Museo Nazionale Romano: Palazzo Massimo alle Terme*

⊙ *Colosseum*

⊙ *Basilica di San Giovanni in Laterano*

Aventino & Testaccio (p108)

Ideal for a romantic getaway, hilltop Aventino rises above Testaccio, famous for its nose-to-tail cooking and thumping nightlife.

San Giovanni & Celio (p96)

Explore medieval churches and escape the tourist crowds in residential San Giovanni and on the leafy Celio hill.

⊙ Top Sights

Basilica di San Giovanni in Laterano

⊙ *Appian Way*

Worth a Trip

⊙ Top Sights

Appian Way

Villa Borghese

Explore
Rome

Worth a Trip

View from the Colosseum (p24) to Arco di Costantino
RPBAIAO/SHUTTERSTOCK ©

Explore

Ancient Rome

In a city of extraordinary beauty, Rome's ancient heart stands out.
It's here you'll find the great icons of the city's past: the Colosseum;
the Palatino; the forums; and the Campidoglio (Capitoline Hill), the
historic home of the Capitoline Museums. Touristy by day, it's quiet
at night with few after-hours attractions.

The Sights in a Day

☀ Start early at the **Colosseum** (p24), Rome's fearsome gladiatorial arena. Your ticket for the Colosseum also covers admission to the Palatino and the Roman Forum, so make the **Palatino** (p31) your next stop. Explore the spot where Romulus supposedly founded the city and visit the **Orti Farnesiani** (p31) for wonderful views over the **Roman Forum** (p26), which is your next stop.

☼ Next, visit the **Capitoline Museums** (p32) for their fine collection of classical sculpture. Before going in, stop for a *panini* at the museum cafe, **Terrazza Caffarelli** (p34). Stroll through the **Piazza del Campidoglio** (p32) on the way to **Chiesa di Santa Maria Antiqua** (p32), the oldest Christian monument in the forum. Take a break from history to head to the top of the **Vittoriano** (p33) for amazing views over Rome. If you've still got an appetite for archaeology, squeeze in one more ruin – the **Imperial Forums** (p32). For more insight into these buildings, include the **Mercati di Traiano Museo dei Fori Imperiali** (p32).

☾ Sightseeing over for the day, enjoy a dinner of traditional Roman fare at **Terre e Domus** (p33). End the evening with a beer at **BrewDog Roma** (p34).

👁 Top Sights

Colosseum (p24)

Roman Forum (p26)

🖤 Best of Rome

History

Colosseum (p24)

Roman Forum (p26)

Palatino (p31)

Bocca della Verità (p33)

Architecture

Colosseum (p24)

Mercati di Traiano Museo dei Fori Imperiali (p32)

Piazza del Campidoglio (p32)

Getting There

🚌 **Bus** In the northwest of the neighbourhood Piazza Venezia is an important hub. Many services stop in or near here, including numbers 40, 64, 87, 170, 916 and H.

Ⓜ **Metro** Metro line B has stations at the Colosseum (Colosseo) and Circo Massimo. If taking the metro at Termini follow signs for Line B direzione Laurentina.

Top Sights
Colosseum

An awesome, spine-tingling sight, the Colosseum is the most thrilling of Rome's ancient monuments. It was here that gladiators met in mortal combat and condemned prisoners fought off wild beasts in front of baying, bloodthirsty crowds. Two thousand years on and it's one of Italy's top tourist attractions, drawing more than six million visitors a year.

The Exterior
The outer walls have three levels of arches, framed by decorative columns topped by capitals

⊙ Map p30, D4

☎ 06 3996 7700

www.coopculture.it

Piazza del Colosseo

adult/reduced incl Roman Forum & Palatino €12/7.50

🕒 8.30am-1hr before sunset

Ⓜ Colosseo

Arena of the Colosseum

of the Ionic (at the bottom), Doric and Corinthian (at the top) orders. They were originally covered in travertine and marble statues filled the niches on the 2nd and 3rd storeys. The 80 entrance arches, known as *vomitoria*, allowed the spectators to enter and be seated in a matter of minutes.

The Arena

The stadium originally had a wooden floor covered in sand – *harena* in Latin, hence the word 'arena' – to prevent combatants from slipping and to soak up spilt blood.

Hypogeum

The hypogeum served as the stadium's backstage area. It was here that stage sets were prepared and combatants, both human and animal, would gather before show time. Trapdoors led up to the arena. To hoist people, animals and scenery up to the arena, the hypogeum had a sophisticated network of 80 winch-operated lifts, all controlled by a single pulley system.

The Seating

The *cavea,* for spectator seating, was divided into three tiers: magistrates and senior officials sat in the lowest tier, wealthy citizens in the middle and the plebs in the highest tier. Women (except for vestal virgins) were relegated to the cheapest sections at the top. And as in modern stadiums, tickets were numbered and spectators were assigned a precise seat in a specific sector – in 2015, restorers uncovered traces of red numerals on the arches, indicating how the sectors were numbered. The podium, a broad terrace in front of the tiers of seats, was reserved for the emperor, senators and VIPs.

☑ Top Tips

▶ Visit in the early morning or late afternoon to avoid the crowds.

▶ If queues are long, get your ticket at the Palatino, about 250m away at Via di San Gregorio 30.

▶ Other queue-jumping tips: book your ticket online at www.coopculture.it (plus a €2 booking fee); get the Roma Pass; or join an official English-language tour (€5 on top of the regular ticket price).

▶ The hypogeum, along with the top tier, can be visited on a guided tour. This must be booked in advance and costs €9 plus the normal Colosseum ticket.

✕ Take a Break

Avoid the rip-off restaurants in the near vicinity and head east of the Colosseum for a light, casual meal at Cafè Cafè (p103).

Top Sights
Roman Forum

The Roman Forum (Foro Romano) was ancient Rome's showpiece centre, a grandiose district of temples, basilicas and vibrant public spaces. Nowadays, it's a collection of impressive, if sketchily labelled, ruins that can leave you drained and confused. But if you can get your imagination going, there's something wonderfully compelling about walking in the footsteps of Julius Caesar and other legendary figures of Roman history.

👁 Map p30, C3

📞 06 3996 7700

www.coopculture.it

Largo della Salara Vecchia, Piazza di Santa Maria Nova

adult/reduced incl Colosseum & Palatino €12/7.50

🕐 8.30am–1hr before sunset

🚍 Via dei Fori Imperiali

Arco di Settimio Severo

Via Sacra

Via Sacra, the Roman Forum's main thoroughfare, traverses the site from northwest to southeast. In ancient times, victorious military campaigns would often be celebrated with a dramatic procession (a Triumph) up Via Sacra to Capitoline Hill.

Curia

The Via Sacra brings you to the Curia, the meeting place of the Roman Senate. The construction you see today is a 1937 reconstruction of the building as it looked in the 3rd-century reign of Diocletian. In front of the Curia, and hidden by scaffolding, is the Lapis Niger, a large piece of black marble that's said to cover the tomb of Romulus.

Arco di Settimio Severo

At the end of Via Sacra stands this 23m-high monument. Dedicated to the eponymous emperor and his two sons, it was built in AD 203 to celebrate the Roman victory over the Parthians.

Rostri

An elaborate podium overlooking what was the Piazza del Foro, this is where Shakespeare had Mark Antony make his famous 'Friends, Romans, countrymen...' monologue, and where politicians would stand to pontificate to the crowds below. Its name is a reference to the bronze beaks (rostri, or rostra in Latin), spoils from the battle of Antium in 338 BC, used to decorate the giant platform.

Colonna di Foca

Facing the Rostri, the Colonna di Foca marks the centre of Piazza del Foro. The last monument erected in the Roman Forum, it was built in honour of the Eastern Roman emperor Phocus in 608.

Tempio di Saturno

Eight granite columns are all that remain of the Tempio di Saturno, one of the Roman Forum's

---

☑ Top Tips

▶ Get grandstand views of the Forum from the Palatino and Campidoglio. Alternatively, head up to the viewing platform at the top of the Rampa imperiale.

▶ Visit first thing in the morning or late afternoon; crowds are worst between 11am and 2pm.

▶ In summer it gets very hot in the Forum and there's little shade, so take a hat and plenty of water.

▶ If you're caught short, there are toilets by the Chiesa di Santa Maria Antiqua.

✗ Take a Break

For a restorative coffee break, head up to the Campidoglio and the Terrazza Caffarelli (p34), the Capitoline Museums' panoramic rooftop cafe.

If you want something more substantial, search out Terre e Domus (p33) which serves excellent regional cuisine and fine local wines.

200 m
0.1 miles

Via Cavour

Via del Colosseo

Via del Tempio della Pace

Largo C Ricci

Via dei Fori Imperiali

Largo della Salara Vecchia

Entrance

Basilica di Massenzio

Arco di Tito

Entrance

Tempio di Antonino e Faustina

Tempio di Romolo

Via Sacra

Basilica Fulvia Aemilia

Via della Salara Vecchia

Tempio di Giulio Cesare

Casa delle Vestali

Orti Farnesiani

Via della Curia

Via di Tulliano

Piazza del Foro

Via Sacra

Tempio di Castore e Polluce

Tempio di Vesta

Chiesa di Santa Maria Antiqua

Rampa imperiale

Arco di Settimio Severo

Lapis Niger

Rostri

Colonna di Foca

Basilica Giulia

Vicus Tuscus

Via del Foro Romano

Via di San Pietro in Carcere

Entrance

Tempio della Concordia

Tempio di Vespasiano

Tempio di Saturno

Portico degli Dei Consenti

Via dei Fienili

Via dei Foraggi

Piazza del Campidoglio

Arco di Tito

landmark sights. Inaugurated in 497 BC and subsequently rebuilt in the 1st century BC, it was an important temple that doubled as the state treasury.

Tempio di Castore e Polluce

In the centre of the Roman Forum, three Corinthian columns survive from the Tempio di Castore e Polluce. This temple, dedicated to the heavenly twins Castor and Pollux, was built in 484 BC to celebrate the defeat of the Latin League in 496 BC.

Casa delle Vestali

The Casa delle Vestali was home to the virgins who tended the sacred flame in the adjoining Tempio di Vesta. The six priestesses were selected from patrician families when aged between six and 10 to serve in the temple for 30 years. If the flame in the temple went out, the priestess responsible would be flogged.

Basilica di Massenzio

This hulking construction is the largest building on the Roman Forum. Started by the Emperor Maxentius and finished by Constantine in 315, it originally covered an area of approximately 100m by 65m.

Arco di Tito

Said to be the inspiration for Paris' Arc de Triomphe, the well-preserved Arch of Titus was built in AD 81 to celebrate Vespasian and Titus' victories against Jerusalem.

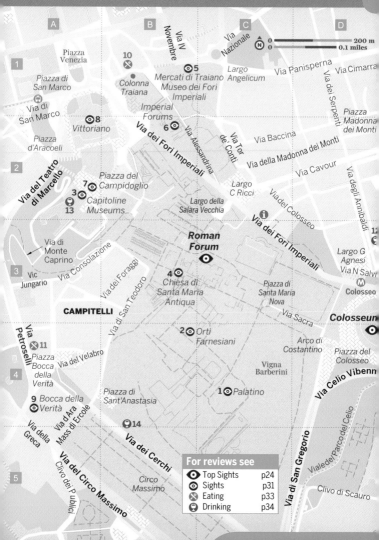

A

B

C

D

Piazza Venezia

Via IV Novembre

Via Nazionale

0   200 m
0   0.1 miles

Piazza di San Marco

10 ✗

Colonna Traiana

Largo Angelicum

Via Panisperna

Via Cimarra

Via dei Serpenti

Via di San Marco

5 ⊙
Mercati di Traiano
Museo dei Fori
Imperiali

Piazza Madonna dei Monti

Piazza d'Aracoeli

8 ⊙
Vittoriano

Imperial Forums

6 ⊙

Via dei Fori Imperiali

Via Alessandrina

Via Tor de' Conti

Via Baccina

Via della Madonna dei Monti

Via Cavour

Via degli Annibaldi

Via del Teatro di Marcello

7 ⊙
Piazza del Campidoglio

3 ⊙
13 ⊙
Capitoline Museums

Largo della Salara Vecchia

Largo C Ricci

Via del Colosseo

Via dei Fori Imperiali

12

Via di Monte Caprino

Via di San Teodoro

Roman Forum ⊙

Largo G Agnesi
Via N Salvi

ⓂColosseo

Vic Jungario

Via Consolazione

Via dei Foraggi

4 ⊙
Chiesa di Santa Maria Antiqua

Piazza di Santa Maria Nova

Via Sacra

Colosseum ⊙

CAMPITELLI

11 ✗

Via del Velabro

2 ⊙ Orti Farnesiani

Arco di Costantino

Vigna Barberini

Piazza del Colosseo

Via Celio Vibenn

Via Petroselli

Piazza Bocca della Verità

9 ⊙ Bocca della Verità

Piazza di Sant'Anastasia

1 ⊙ Palatino

Via d'Ara Mass di Ercole

14 ✗

Via dei Cerchi

Via San Gregorio

Viale del Parco del Celio

Via della Greca

Via del Circo Massimo

Clivo del P ublic

Circo Massimo

Clivo di Scauro

The Palatino

Sights

Palatino
ARCHAEOLOGICAL SITE

1 ◉ Map p30, C4

Sandwiched between the Roman Forum and the Circo Massimo, the Palatino (Palatine Hill) is an atmospheric area of towering pine trees, majestic ruins and memorable views. It was here that Romulus supposedly founded the city in 753 BC and Rome's emperors lived in unabashed luxury. Look out for the **stadio** (Stadium; Via di San Gregorio 30, Palatino; Ⓜ Colosseo), the ruins of the **Domus Flavia** (Imperial Palace; Via di San Gregorio 30, Palatino; Ⓜ Colosseo), and grandstand views over the Roman Forum from the Orti Farnesiani. (Palatine Hill; ☎ 06 3996 7700; www.coopculture.it; Via di San Gregorio 30, Piazza di Santa Maria Nova; adult/reduced incl Colosseum & Roman Forum €12/7.50; ⏱ 8.30am-1hr before sunset; Ⓜ Colosseo)

Orti Farnesiani
GARDENS

2 ◉ Map p30, B4

On the Palatino Hill, the 16th-century Orti Farnesiani is one of Europe's earliest botanical gardens. A viewing balcony at the northern point of the garden commands breathtaking views over the Roman Forum. (Via di San Gregorio 30, Palatino; Ⓜ Colosseo)

Capitoline Museums
MUSEUM

3 ◉ Map p30, A2

Dating to 1471, the Capitoline Museums are the world's oldest public museums. Their collection of classical sculpture is one of Italy's finest, including crowd-pleasers such as the iconic *Lupa capitolina* (Capitoline Wolf), a sculpture of Romulus and Remus under a wolf, and the *Galata morente* (Dying Gaul), a moving depiction of a dying Gaul warrior. There's also a formidable picture gallery with masterpieces by the likes of Titian, Tintoretto, Rubens and Caravaggio. Ticket prices increase when there's a temporary exhibition on. (Musei Capitolini; ☏06 06 08; www.museicapitolini.org; Piazza del Campidoglio 1; adult/reduced €11.50/9.50; ⊙9.30am-7.30pm, last admission 6.30pm; 🚇Piazza Venezia)

Chiesa di Santa Maria Antiqua
CHURCH

4 ◉ Map p30, B3

This ancient church, the oldest and most important Christian monument in the Roman Forum, is a unique treasure trove of early Christian art. Its cavernous interior, recently opened after a 30-year restoration, is lined with exquisite 6th- to 9th-century frescoes. Particularly impressive is an image on the east wall showing Christ with the fathers of the Eastern and Western churches and a hanging depiction of the Virgin Mary with child, one of the earliest icons in existence. (Largo della Salara Vecchia, Roman Forum; ⊙currently closed; 🚇Via dei Fori Imperiali)

Mercati di Traiano Museo dei Fori Imperiali
MUSEUM

5 ◉ Map p30, B1

This striking museum brings to life the Mercati di Traiano, emperor Trajan's great 2nd-century complex, while also providing a fascinating introduction to the Imperial Forums (p32) with multimedia displays, explanatory panels and a smattering of archaeological artefacts. (☏06 06 08; www.mercatiditraiano.it; Via IV Novembre 94; adult/reduced €11.50/9.50; ⊙9.30am-7.30pm, last admission 6.30pm; 🚇Via IV Novembre)

Imperial Forums
ARCHAEOLOGICAL SITE

6 ◉ Map p30, B2

Visible from Via dei Fori Imperiali and, when it's open, Via Alessandrina, the forums of Trajan, Augustus, Nerva and Caesar are known collectively as the Imperial Forums. These were largely buried when Mussolini bulldozed Via dei Fori Imperiali through the area in 1933, but excavations have since unearthed much of them. The standout sights are the Mercati di Traiano (Trajan's Markets), accessible through the Museo dei Fori Imperiali, and the landmark Colonna Traiana (Trajan's Column). (Fori Imperiali; Via dei Fori Imperiali; 🚇Via dei Fori Imperiali)

Piazza del Campidoglio
PIAZZA

7 ◉ Map p30, A2

This hilltop piazza, designed by Michelangelo in 1538, is one of Rome's most beautiful squares. There are several approaches but the most dramatic is via the graceful **Cordonata** (Piazza d'Aracoeli) staircase up from Piazza d'Aracoeli. The piazza is flanked by Palazzo Nuovo and Palazzo dei Conservatori, together home to the Capitoline Museums, and Palazzo Senatorio, the seat of Rome city council. In the centre is a copy of an equestrian statue of Marcus Aurelius. (🚊 Piazza Venezia)

Vittoriano   MONUMENT

🔘 8 ⊙ Map p30, A2

Love it or loathe it, as many Romans do, you can't ignore the Vittoriano (aka the Altare della Patria, Altar of the Fatherland), the massive mountain of white marble that towers over Piazza Venezia. Begun in 1885 to honour Italy's first king, Victor Emmanuel II – who's immortalised in its vast equestrian statue – it incorporates the **Museo Centrale del Risorgimento** (📞06 679 35 98; www.risorgimento.it; adult/reduced €5/2.50; ⊙9.30am-6.30pm; 🚊 Piazza Venezia), a small museum documenting Italian unification, and the **Tomb of the Unknown Soldier**.

For Rome's best 360-degree views, take the **Roma dal Cielo** (adult/reduced €7/3.50; ⊙9.30am-7.30pm, last entry 7pm; 🚊 Piazza Venezia) lift to the top. (Victor Emmanuel Monument; Piazza Venezia; admission free; ⊙9.30am-5.30pm summer, to 4.30pm winter; 🚊 Piazza Venezia)

Bocca della Verità   MONUMENT

🔘 9 ⊙ Map p30, A4

A bearded face carved into a giant marble disc, the *Bocca della Verità* is one of Rome's most popular curiosities. Legend has it that if you put your hand in the mouth and tell a lie, the Bocca will slam shut and bite your hand off. The mouth, which was originally part of a fountain, or possibly an ancient manhole cover, now lives in the portico of the Chiesa di Santa Maria in Cosmedin, a handsome medieval church. (Mouth of Truth; Piazza Bocca della Verità 18; ⊙9.30am-5.50pm; 🚊 Piazza Bocca della Verità)

Eating

Terre e Domus   LAZIO CUISINE €€

🔘 10 ✖ Map p30, B1

This modern white-and-glass restaurant is the best option in the touristy Forum area. With minimal decor and large windows overlooking the

Colonna di Traiano, it's a relaxed spot to sit down to traditional local staples, all made with ingredients sourced from the surrounding Lazio region, and a glass or two of regional wine. (☏06 6994 0273; Via Foro Traiano 82-4; meals €30; ⊘9am-midnight Mon & Wed-Sat, 10am-midnight Sun; ☐Via dei Fori Imperiali)

Ristorante Roof Garden Circus
RISTORANTE €€€

11 🍽 Map p30, A4

The rooftop of the Forty Seven hotel sets the romantic stage for chef Giacomo Tasca's seasonal menu of classic Roman dishes and contemporary Mediterranean cuisine. With the Aventino hill rising in the background, you can tuck into stalwarts such as spaghetti *ajo e ojio* (with garlic and olive oil) or opt for something richer like fillet of beef with zucchini, peppermint and roasted peppers. (☏06 678 78 16; www.fortysevenhotel.com; Via Petroselli 47, Hotel Forty Seven; meals €60; ⊘noon-10.30pm; ☐Via Petroselli)

Drinking

BrewDog Roma
CRAFT BEER

12 🍺 Map p30, D3

This new bar by Scottish brewery Brew-Dog has proved a hit with Rome's craft-beer lovers since opening in the shadow of the Colosseum in late 2015. With a stripped-down brick look and up to 20 brews on tap, it's a fine spot to kick back after a day on the sights. (☏392 9308655; www.brewdog.com/bars/worldwide/roma; Via delle Terme di Tito 80; ⊘noon-1am Sun-Thu, to 2am Fri & Sat; Ⓜ Colosseo)

Terrazza Caffarelli
CAFE

13 🍺 Map p30, A2

The Capitoline Museums' stylish terrace cafe is a memorable place to relax over a drink or light lunch (*panini,* salads, pastas) and swoon over magical views of the city's domes and rooftops. Although part of the museum complex, you don't need a ticket to come here as it has an independent entrance on Piazzale Caffarelli. (Caffetteria dei Musei Capitolini; ☏06 6919 0564; Piazzale Caffarelli 4; ⊘9.30am-7pm; ☐Piazza Venezia)

0,75
BAR

14 🍺 Map p30, B4

This welcoming bar overlooking the Circo Massimo is good for a lingering evening drink, an *aperitivo* or casual meal (mains €6 to €16.50). It's a friendly place with a laid-back vibe, an international crowd, attractive wood-beam look and cool tunes. (☏06 687 57 06; www.075roma.com; Via dei Cerchi 65; ⊘11am-2am; 🛜; ☐Via dei Cerchi)

Understand

A Who's Who of Roman Emperors

Of the 250 or so emperors of the Roman Empire, only a few were truly heroic. Here are 10 of the best, worst and completely insane.

Augustus (27 BC–AD 14) Rome's first emperor. Ushers in a period of peace and security; the arts flourish and many monuments are built.

Caligula (37–41) Emperor number three after Augustus and Tiberius. Remains popular until illness leads to the depraved behaviour for which he becomes infamous. Is murdered by his bodyguards on the Palatino.

Claudius (41–54) Expands the Roman Empire and conquers Britain. Is eventually poisoned, probably at the instigation of Agrippina, his wife and Nero's mother.

Nero (54–68) Initially rules well but later slips into madness – he has his mother murdered, persecutes the Christians and attempts to turn half the city into a palace, the Domus Aurea. He is eventually forced into suicide.

Vespasian (69–79) First of the Flavian dynasty, he imposes peace and cleans up the imperial finances. His greatest legacy is the Colosseum.

Trajan (98–117) Conquers the east and rules over the empire at its zenith. He revamps Rome's city centre, adding a forum, marketplace and column, all of which still stand.

Hadrian (117–38) Puts an end to imperial expansion and constructs walls to mark the empire's borders.

Aurelian (270–75) Does much to control the rebellion that sweeps the empire at the end of the 3rd century. Starts construction of the city walls that still today bear his name.

Diocletian (284–305) Splits the empire into eastern and western halves in 285. Launches a savage persecution of the Christians as he struggles to control the empire's eastern reaches.

Constantine I (306–37) Although based in Byzantium (later renamed Constantinople in his honour), he legalises Christianity.

Explore

Centro Storico

A tightly packed tangle of animated piazzas, cobbled alleys, Renaissance *palazzi* (mansions) and baroque churches, the historic centre is the Rome many come to find. Its romantic streets teem with boutiques, cafes, restaurants and stylish bars, while market traders and street artists work the crowds on the vibrant squares.

The Sights in a Day

☀️ Rome's historic centre is made for leisurely strolling. Kick-start your explorations with an espresso from **Caffè Sant'Eustachio** (p49), then beat the crowds to the **Pantheon** (p38). Next, nip down to the **Basilica di Santa Maria Sopra Minerva** (p45) to glimpse a minor Michelangelo before heading to the **Galleria Doria Pamphilj** (p44) and its superb collection of Old Masters. That done, stop in at **Chiesa del Gesu** (p44) on your way to lunch at **La Ciambella** (p47).

☀️ Recharged, push on to **Piazza Navona** (p44; pictured left), Rome's showpiece baroque square. Nearby, the **Museo Nazionale Romano: Palazzo Altemps** (p44) houses some wonderful classical sculpture and the **Chiesa di San Luigi dei Francesi** (p45) boasts a trio of Caravaggios. To round off the day's sightseeing check out **Campo de' Fiori** (p51).

🌙 Dine on delicious pizza at **Emma Pizzeria** (p47), before treating yourself to gelati at **Gelateria del Teatro** (p48). Cap off the night at one of the area's many bars – try the **Gin Corner** (p50) for cocktails.

For a local's day in the Centro Storico, see p40.

👁 Top Sight
Pantheon (p38)

🔍 Local Life
A Day Out in the Centro Storico (p40)

❤ Best of Rome
History
Pantheon (p38)

Chiesa del Gesù (p44)

Teatro Argentina (p51)

Food
Armando al Pantheon (p48)

Gelateria del Teatro (p48)

Getting There

🚌 **Bus** The best way to access the *centro storico*. A whole fleet serves the area from Termini, including numbers 40 and 64, which both stop at Largo di Torre Argentina and continue down Corso Vittorio Emanuele II. From Via del Tritone near Barberini metro station, bus 492 runs to Corso del Rinascimento for Piazza Navona.

Ⓜ **Metro** There are no metro stations in the neighbourhood but it's within walking distance of Barberini, Spagna and Flaminio stations, all on line A.

🚊 **Tram** Number 8 runs from Piazza Venezia to Trastevere by way of Via Arenula.

Top Sights
Pantheon

A striking 2000-year-old temple, now a church, the Pantheon is Rome's best-preserved ancient monument and one of the most influential buildings in the Western world. Its greying, pock-marked exterior might look its age, but inside it's a different story, and it's a unique and exhilarating experience to pass through its vast bronze doors and gaze up at the largest unreinforced concrete dome ever built.

👁 Map p42, C3

www.pantheonroma.com

Piazza della Rotonda

admission free

🕐 8.30am-7.15pm Mon-Sat, 9am-5.45pm Sun

🚊 Largo di Torre Argentina

Oculus and dome

The Exterior

Originally, the Pantheon was on a raised podium, its entrance facing onto a rectangular porticoed piazza. Nowadays, the dark-grey pitted exterior faces onto busy, cafe-lined Piazza della Rotonda. And while its facade is somewhat the worse for wear, it's still an imposing sight. The monumental entrance portico consists of 16 Corinthian columns, each 11.8m high and each made from a single block of Egyptian granite.

The Interior

Although impressive from outside, it's only when you get inside that you can really appreciate the Pantheon's full size. With light streaming in through the oculus (the 8.7m-diameter hole in the centre of the dome), the cylindrical marble-clad interior seems vast, an effect that was deliberately designed to cut worshippers down to size in the face of the gods.

Opposite the entrance is the church's main altar, over which hangs a 7th-century icon of the *Madonna col Bambino* (Madonna and Child). To the left (as you look in from the entrance) is the tomb of Raphael, marked by Lorenzetto's 1520 sculpture of the *Madonna del Sasso* (Madonna of the Rock).

The Dome

The Pantheon's dome, considered the Romans' most important architectural achievement, was the largest dome in the world until the 15th century when Brunelleschi beat it with his Florentine cupola. Its harmonious appearance is due to a precisely calibrated symmetry – its diameter is exactly equal to the building's interior height of 43.4m. At its centre, the oculus, which symbolically connected the temple with the gods, plays a vital structural role by absorbing and redistributing the dome's huge tensile forces.

☑ **Top Tips**

▶ The Pantheon is a working church and mass is celebrated at 5pm on Saturday and 10.30am on Sunday.

▶ Visit around midday to see a beam of sunlight stream in through the oculus.

▶ Look down as well as up – the sloping marble floor has 22 almost-invisible holes to drain away the rain that gets in through the oculus.

▶ Return after dark for amazing views of the building set against the ink-blue night sky.

✕ **Take a Break**

The streets around the Pantheon are thick with trattorias, cafes and bars. For an uplifting espresso, try the nearby La Casa del Caffè Tazza d'Oro (p50), one of Rome's finest coffee houses.

To escape the crowds and have a great plate of pasta, look up La Ciambella (p47), a relaxed all-day eatery in a quiet side street.

Local Life
A Day Out in the Centro Storico

Rome's historic centre casts a powerful spell. But it's not just visitors who fall for its romantic piazzas, suggestive lanes, and streetside cafes. Away from the tourist spotlight, locals love to spend time here, shopping, unwinding over a drink, taking in an exhibition or simply hanging out with friends.

❶ An Exhibition at the Chiostro del Bramante

Tucked away in the backstreets near Piazza Navona, the Renaissance **Chiostro del Bramante** (www.chiostrodel bramante.it; Via Arco della Pace 5; exhibitions adult/reduced €13/11; ⊙ church 9am-11.45pm Mon, Wed & Sat, cloister 10am-8pm Mon-Fri, to 9pm Sat & Sun; 🚍 Corso del Rinascimento) is a stunning setting for modern-art

exhibitions. Afterwards, pop upstairs for a coffee, light lunch or drink at the smart in-house cafe.

➋ Shopping around Via del Governo Vecchio

A charming street lined with arty boutiques, **Via del Governo Vecchio** (🚇Corso Vittorio Emanuele II) strikes off Piazza Pasquino, home to a celebrated 'talking statue' (to which Romans used to stick notes lampooning the authorities). It can get touristy but locals love the vibe too and the area has some great shops, including trendy jeans store **SBU** (📞06 6880 2547; www.sbu.it; Via di San Pantaleo 68-69; ⏲10am-7.30pm Mon-Sat; 🚇Corso Vittorio Emanuele II).

➌ Lunch at Alfredo e Ada

For an authentic trattoria meal, search out the much-loved **Alfredo e Ada** (📞06 687 8842; Via dei Banchi Nuovi 14; meals €25-30; ⏲noon-3pm & 7-10pm Tue-Sat; 🚇Corso Vittorio Emanuele II). It's distinctly no-frills with spindly, marble-topped tables and homey clutter, but there's a warm, friendly atmosphere and the traditional Roman food is filling and flavoursome.

➍ Stroll Via Giulia

Lined with Renaissance *palazzi* and potted orange trees, **Via Giulia** is a picture-perfect strip to stroll. At its southern end, the Fontana del Mascherone depicts a gobsmacked 17th-century hippie spewing water from his mouth. Close by, the overhead Arco Farnese was part of an ambitious, unfinished project to link two Farnese palaces.

➎ An Optical Illusion at Palazzo Spada

Largely bypassed by the sightseeing hordes, **Palazzo Spada** (Palazzo Capodiferro; 📞06 683 2409; http://galleriaspada. beniculturali.it; Piazza Capo di Ferro 13; adult/reduced €5/2.50; ⏲8.30am-7.30pm Wed-Mon; 🚇Corso Vittorio Emanuele II) is home to a celebrated illusion, Borromini's *Prospettiva* (Perspective). What appears to be a 25m-long corridor lined with columns leading to a hedge and life-sized statue is, in fact, only 10m long, and the sculpture, a later addition, is actually hip-height.

➏ Beer at Open Baladin

Rome's craft beer scene is now well established and with more than 40 brew on tap and up to 100 bottled beers, **Open Baladin** (📞06 683 8989; www.openbaladinroma.it; Via degli Specchi 6; ⏲noon-2am; 🛜; 🚇Via Arenula) is one of its leading lights. A cool, modern pub near Campo de' Fiori, it specialises in Italian brews, many from small microbreweries.

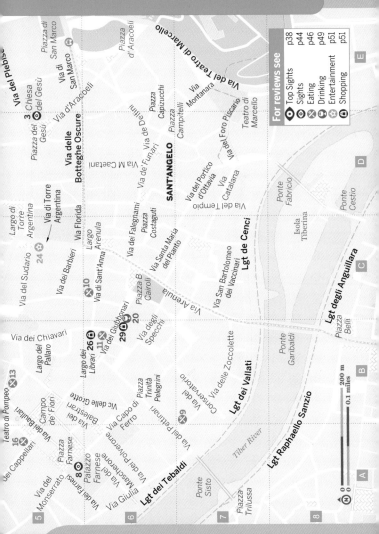

For reviews see

◉ Top Sights	p38
◎ Sights	p44
✕ Eating	p46
🍷 Drinking	p49
✿ Entertainment	p51
🛍 Shopping	p51

Piazza di San Marco

Piazza d'Aracoeli

Via del Plebiscito

Chiesa del Gesù **3**

Piazza del Gesù

Via di San Marco

Via d'Aracoeli

Via del Teatro di Marcello

Via delle Botteghe Oscure

Via M Caetani

Via de Delfini

Via Montanara

Piazza Capizucchi

Piazza Campitelli

Via di Torre Argentina

Largo di Torre Argentina

24 ✿

Via del Sudario

Via Florida

Via dei Falegnami

Via de Funari

SANT'ANGELO

Piazza Costaguti

Via del Foro Piscario

Teatro di Marcello

Via del Portico d'Ottavia

Via Catalana

Via del Tempio

Via dei Barberi

Via Arenula

Largo Arenula

Via di Sant'Anna

Piazza B Cairoli

Via Santa Maria del Pianto

Via San Bartolomeo dei Vaccinari

Lgt de Cenci

Ponte Fabricio

Isola Tiberina

Ponte Cestio

✕ **10**

Via Arenula

Lgt degli Anguillara

Via dei Chiavari

Largo del Pallaro

Largo dei Librari **26** 🏠

11 ✕ **29** ✕

Via dei Giubbonari

20

Via degli Specchi

Piazza Belli

Ponte Garibaldi

✕ **13**

Teatro di Pompeo

dei Cappellari

16 ✕

Via dei Baullari

Campo de' Fiori

Piazza Farnese

Palazzo Farnese ◉ **8**

Via del Monserrato

Via dei Farnesi

Via del Mascherone

Via di Pevierone

Via Giulia

Via di Capo di Ferro

Piazza Trinità Pelegrini

Vic delle Grotte

Via dei Balestrari

66 ✕

Via del Pellegrini

Via del Conservatorio

Via delle Zoccolette

Lgt dei Vallati

Lgt Raphaello Sanzio

Tiber River

Ponte Sisto

Piazza Trilussa

Lgt dei Tebaldi

200 m
0.1 miles

A | B | C | D | E
5 | 6 | 7 | 8

Sights

Piazza Navona   PIAZZA

1 🎯 Map p42, B3

With its showy fountains, baroque *palazzi* (mansions) and colourful cast of street artists, hawkers and tourists, Piazza Navona is central Rome's elegant showcase square. Built over the 1st-century **Stadio di Domiziano** (Domitian's Stadium; 📞06 4568 6100; www.stadiodomiziano.com; Via di Tor Sanguigna 3; adult/reduced €8/6; ⏰10am-7pm Sun-Fri, to 8pm Sat), it was paved over in the 15th century and for almost 300 years hosted the city's main market. Its grand centrepiece is Bernini's **Fontana dei Quattro Fiumi** (Fountain of the Four Rivers), a flamboyant fountain featuring an Egyptian obelisk and muscular personifications of the rivers Nile, Ganges, Danube and Plate. (🚇Corso del Rinascimento)

Galleria Doria Pamphilj   GALLERY

2 🎯 Map p42, E4

Hidden behind the grimy grey exterior of Palazzo Doria Pamphilj, this wonderful gallery boasts one of Rome's richest private art collections, with works by Raphael, Tintoretto, Titian, Caravaggio, Bernini and Velázquez, as well as several Flemish masters. Masterpieces abound, but the undisputed star is Velázquez' portrait of an implacable Pope Innocent X, who grumbled that the depiction was 'too real'. For a comparison, check out Gian Lorenzo Bernini's sculptural interpretation of the same subject. (📞06 679 73 23; www.doriapamphilj.it; Via del Corso 305; adult/reduced €12/8; ⏰9am-7pm, last entry 6pm; 🚇Via del Corso)

Chiesa del Gesù   CHURCH

3 🎯 Map p42, D5

An imposing example of Counter-Reformation architecture, Rome's most important Jesuit church is a fabulous treasure trove of baroque art. Headline works include a swirling vault fresco by Giovanni Battista Gaulli (aka Il Baciccia), and Andrea del Pozzo's opulent tomb for Ignatius Loyola, the Spanish soldier and saint who founded the Jesuits in 1540. St Ignatius lived in the church from 1544 until his death in 1556 and you can visit his private rooms to the right of the main building in the Cappella di Sant'Ignazio. (📞06 69 7001; www.chiesadelgesu.org; Piazza del Gesù; ⏰7am-12.30pm & 4-7.45pm, St Ignatius rooms 4-6pm Mon-Sat, 10am-noon Sun; 🚇Largo di Torre Argentina)

Museo Nazionale Romano: Palazzo Altemps   MUSEUM

4 🎯 Map p42, B2

Just north of Piazza Navona, Palazzo Altemps is a beautiful late-15th-century *palazzo*, housing the best of the Museo Nazionale Romano's formidable collection of classical sculpture. Many pieces come from the celebrated Ludovisi collection, amassed by Cardinal Ludovico Ludovisi in the 17th century. (📞06 3996 7700; www.coopculture.

Interior of the Chiesa del Gesù

it; Piazza Sant'Apollinare 44; adult/reduced €7/3.50; ⏰9am-7.45pm Tue-Sun; 🚇Corso del Rinascimento)

Chiesa di San Luigi dei Francesi
CHURCH

5 💿 Map p42, C3

Church to Rome's French community since 1589, this opulent baroque *chiesa* is home to a celebrated trio of Caravaggio paintings: the *Vocazione di San Matteo* (The Calling of Saint Matthew), the *Martirio di San Matteo* (The Martyrdom of Saint Matthew) and *San Matteo e l'angelo* (Saint Matthew and the Angel), known collectively as the St Matthew cycle. (Piazza di San Luigi dei Francesi 5; ⏰9.30am-12.45pm & 2.30-6.30pm Mon-Fri, 9.30am-12.15pm & 2.30-6.45pm Sat, 11.30am-12.45pm & 2.30-6.45pm Sun; 🚇Corso del Rinascimento)

Basilica di Santa Maria Sopra Minerva
BASILICA

6 💿 Map p42, D4

Built on the site of three pagan temples, including one dedicated to the goddess Minerva, the Dominican Basilica di Santa Maria Sopra Minerva is Rome's only Gothic church. However, little remains of the original 13th-century structure and these days the main drawcard is a minor Michelangelo sculpture and the magisterial, art-rich interior. (www.santamaria sopraminerva.it; Piazza della Minerva 42;

⏱6.40am-7pm Mon-Fri, 6.40am-12.30pm & 3.30-7pm Sat, 8am-12.30pm & 3.30-7pm Sun; 🚌Largo di Torre Argentina)

Basilica di Sant'Agostino

BASILICA

7 ◉ Map p42, B2

The plain white facade of this early Renaissance church, built in the 15th century and renovated in the late 1700s, gives no indication of the impressive art inside. The most famous work is Caravaggio's *Madonna dei Pellegrini* (Madonna of the Pilgrims), in the first chapel on the left, but you'll also find a fresco by Raphael and a much-venerated sculpture by Jacopo Sansovino. (Piazza di Sant'Agostino 80; ⏱7.30am-noon & 4-7.30pm; 🚌Corso del Rinascimento)

Top Tip

For Free

The *centro storico* is an expensive part of town but there are ways of making your money go further. You can see masterpieces by the likes of Michelangelo, Raphael, Caravaggio and Bernini for nothing by visiting the area's churches, all of which are free to enter. Save money on bottled water by filling up at the drinking fountains known as *nasoni* (big noses).

Palazzo Farnese

HISTORIC BUILDING

8 ◉ Map p42, A5

Home of the French Embassy, this formidable Renaissance *palazzo,* one of Rome's finest, was started in 1514 by Antonio da Sangallo the Younger, continued by Michelangelo and finished by Giacomo della Porta. Inside, it boasts a series of frescoes by Annibale and Agostino Carracci that are said by some to rival Michelangelo's in the Sistine Chapel. The highlight, painted between 1597 and 1608, is the monumental ceiling fresco *Amori degli Dei* (The Loves of the Gods) in the Galleria dei Carracci. (www.inventerrome. com; Piazza Farnese; €9; ⏱guided tours 3pm, 4pm & 5pm Mon, Wed & Fri; 🚌Corso Vittorio Emanuele II)

Eating

Pianostrada

RISTORANTE €€

9 ✖ Map p42, B7

Hatched in foodie Trastevere but now across the river in a mellow white space with vintage furnishings and glorious summer courtyard, this bistro is a fashionable must. Reserve ahead, or settle for a stool at the bar and enjoy big bold views of the kitchen at work. Cuisine is refreshingly creative, seasonal and veg-packed, including gourmet open sandwiches and sensational homemade focaccia as well as full-blown mains. (📞06 8957 2296; Via delle Zoccolette 22; meals €40; ⏱1-4pm & 7pm-midnight Tue-Fri, 10am-midnight Sat & Sun; 🚌Via Arenula)

Emma Pizzeria

PIZZA €€

10 Map p42, C6

Tucked in behind the Chiesa di San Carlo ai Catinari, this smart, modern pizzeria is a top spot for a cracking pizza and smooth craft beer (or a wine from its pretty extensive list). It's a stylish setup with outdoor seating and a spacious, art-clad interior, and a menu that lists seasonal, wood-fired pizzas alongside classic Roman pastas and mains. (06 6476 0475; www.emmapizzeria.com; Via Monte della Farina 28-29; pizzas €8-18, mains €35; 12.30-3pm & 7-11.30pm; Via Arenula)

Forno Roscioli

PIZZA, BAKERY €

11 Map p42, B6

This is one of Rome's top bakeries, much loved by lunching locals who crowd here for luscious sliced pizza, prize pastries and hunger-sating *supplì* (risotto balls). The *pizza margherita* is superb, if messy to eat, and there's also a counter serving hot pastas and vegetable side dishes. (06 686 4045; www.anticofornoroscioli.it; Via dei Chiavari 34; pizza slices from €2, snacks €2; 6am-8pm Mon-Sat, 9am-7pm Sun; Via Arenula)

La Ciambella

ITALIAN €€

12 Map p42, D4

Central but largely undiscovered by the tourist hordes, this friendly wine-bar-cum-restaurant beats much of the neighbourhood competition. Its spacious, light-filled interior is set over the ruins of the Terme di Agrippa, visible through transparent floor panels, and its kitchen sends out some excellent food, from tartares and chickpea pancakes to slow-cooked beef and traditional Roman pastas. (06 683 2930; www.la-ciambella.it; Via dell'Arco della

Local Life

Jewish Ghetto

Centred on lively Via Portico d'Ottavia, the **Jewish Ghetto** (Lungotevere de' Cenci) is an atmospheric area studded with artisans' studios, vintage clothes shops, kosher bakeries and popular trattorias.

Rome's Jewish community dates back to the 2nd century BC, making it one of the oldest in Europe. The first Jews came to the city as business envoys but many later arrived as slaves following the Roman wars in Judaea and Titus' defeat of Jerusalem in AD 70. Confinement to the Ghetto came in 1555 when Pope Paul IV ushered in a period of official intolerance that lasted, on and off, until the 20th century. Ironically, though, confinement meant that Jewish cultural and religious identity survived intact.

A highlight of the area is the **Teatro di Marcello** (Theatre of Marcellus; Map p42, D7; Via del Teatro di Marcello; Via del Teatro di Marcello), a 20,000-seat mini-Colosseum completed in 11 BC by Augustus.

Ciambella 20; meals €35-45; ⊙bar 7.30am-midnight, wine bar & restaurant noon-11pm Tue-Sun; 🖵Largo di Torre Argentina)

Tiramisù Zum

DESSERTS €

13 🍴 Map p42, B5

The ideal spot for a mid-afternoon pick-me-up, this fab dessert bar specialises in tiramisu, that magnificent marriage of mascarpone and liqueur-soaked ladyfinger biscuits. Choose between the classic version with its cocoa powdering or one of several tempting variations – with pistachio nuts, blackberries and raspberries, and Amarena cherries. (☑06 6830 7836; www.facebook.com/zumroma; Piazza del Teatro di Pompeo 20; desserts €2.50-6; ⊙11am-11.30pm Sun-Thu, to 1am Fri & Sat; 🖵Corso Vittorio Emanuele II)

Armando al Pantheon

ROMAN €€

14 🍴 Map p42, C3

With its cosy wooden interior and unwavering dedication to old-school Roman cuisine, Armando al Pantheon is a regular go-to for local foodies. It's been on the go for more than 50 years and has served its fair share of celebs, but it hasn't let fame go to its head and it remains as popular as ever. Reservations essential. (☑06 6880 3034; www.armandoalpantheon.it; Salita dei Crescenzi 31; meals €40; ⊙12.30-3pm Mon-Sat & 7-11pm Mon-Fri; 🖵Largo di Torre Argentina)

Gelateria del Teatro

GELATO €

15 🍴 Map p42, A2

All the ice cream served at this excellent gelateria is prepared on-site – look through the window and you'll see how. There are about 40 flavours to choose from, all made from thoughtfully sourced ingredients such as hazelnuts from the Langhe region of Piedmont and pistachios from Bronte in Sicily. (☑06 4547 4880; www.gelateriadelteatro.it; Via dei Coronari 65; gelato €2.50-5; ⊙10.30am-8pm winter, 10am-10.30pm summer; 🖵Via Zanardelli)

Forno di Campo de' Fiori

PIZZA, BAKERY €

16 🍴 Map p42, A5

This buzzing bakery on Campo de' Fiori, divided into two adjacent shops, does a roaring trade in *panini* and delicious fresh-from-the-oven *pizza al taglio* (pizza by the slice). Aficionados swear by the *pizza bianca* ('white' pizza with olive oil, rosemary and salt), but the *panini* and *pizza rossa* ('red' pizza, with olive oil, tomato and oregano) taste plenty good too. (www.fornocampodefiori.com; Campo de' Fiori 22; pizza slices around €3; ⊙7.30am-2.30pm & 4.45-8pm Mon-Sat, closed Sat dinner Jul & Aug; 🖵Corso Vittorio Emanuele II)

Casa Bleve

RISTORANTE €€€

17 🍴 Map p42, C4

Ideal for a special occasion dinner, this palatial restaurant-wine-bar dazzles with its column-lined dining hall

Caffè Sant'Eustachio

and stained-glass roof. Its wine list, one of the best in town, accompanies a refined menu of creative antipasti, seasonal pastas and classic main courses. (📞06 686 59 70; www.casableve. it; Via del Teatro Valle 48-49; meals €55-70; 🕐12.30-3pm & 7.30-11pm Mon-Sat; 🚊Largo di Torre Argentina)

Drinking

Barnum Cafe   CAFE

18 🚇 Map p42, A4

A laid-back *Friends*-style cafe, evergreen Barnum is the sort of place you could quickly get used to. With its shabby-chic vintage furniture and white bare-brick walls, it's a relaxed spot for a breakfast cappuccino, a light lunch or a late afternoon drink. Come evening, a coolly dressed-down crowd sips seriously good cocktails. (📞06 6476 0483; www.barnumcafe.com; Via del Pellegrino 87; 🕐9am-10pm Mon, to 2am Tue-Sat; 📶; 🚊Corso Vittorio Emanuele II)

Caffè Sant'Eustachio   COFFEE

19 🚇 Map p42, C4

This small, unassuming cafe, generally three deep at the bar, is reckoned by many to serve the best coffee in town. To make it, the bartenders sneakily beat the first drops of an espresso with several teaspoons of sugar to create a frothy paste to which they add the rest of the coffee. It's superbly smooth and guaranteed to put some zing into your sightseeing.

The chocolate-coated coffee beans sold here are also worth trying. (www.santeustachioilcaffe.it; Piazza Sant'Eustachio 82; ⏰8.30am-1am Sun-Thu, to 1.30am Fri, to 2am Sat; 🚌Corso del Rinascimento)

Roscioli Caffè   CAFE

20 🚇 Map p42, C6

The Roscioli name is a sure bet for good food and drink in this town: the family runs one of Rome's most celebrated **delis** (📞06 687 5287; www.salumeriaroscioli.com; Via dei Giubbonari 21; meals €55; ⏰12.30-4pm & 7pm-midnight Mon-Sat; 🚌Via Arenula) and a hugely popular bakery (p47), and this cafe doesn't disappoint either. The coffee is wonderfully luxurious, and the artfully crafted pastries, petits fours and *panini* taste as good as they look. (📞06 8916 5330; www.rosciolicaffe.com; Piazza Benedetto Cairoli 16; ⏰7am-11pm Mon-Sat, 8am-6pm Sun; 🚌Via Arenula)

Etablì   WINE BAR, CAFE

21 🚇 Map p42, A3

Housed in a 16th-century *palazzo*, Etablì is a rustic-chic lounge-bar-restaurant where you can drop by for a morning coffee, have a light lunch or chat over an *aperitivo*. It's laid-back and good-looking, with original French-inspired country decor – leather armchairs, rough wooden tables and a crackling fireplace. It also

serves full restaurant dinners (€45) and hosts occasional live music. (📞06 9761 6694; www.etabli.it; Vicolo delle Vacche 9a; ⏰cafe 7.30am-6pm, wine bar 6pm-1am; 📶; 🚌Corso del Rinascimento)

La Casa del Caffè Tazza d'Oro   COFFEE

22 🚇 Map p42, D3

A busy, stand-up affair with burnished 1940s fittings, this is one of Rome's best coffee houses. Its espresso hits the mark nicely and there's a range of delicious coffee concoctions, including a cooling *granita di caffè*, a crushed-ice coffee drink served with whipped cream. There's also a small shop and, outside, a coffee *bancomat* for those out-of-hours caffeine emergencies. (📞06 678 9792; www.tazzadorocoffeeshop.com; Via degli Orfani 84-86; ⏰7am-8pm Mon-Sat, 10.30am-7.30pm Sun; 🚌Via del Corso)

Gin Corner   COCKTAIL BAR

23 🚇 Map p42, C1

Forget fine wines and craft beers, this chic bar in the Hotel Adriano is all about the undistilled enjoyment of gin. Here the making of a simple gin and tonic is raised to an art form – the menu lists more than 10 varieties – and martinis are beautifully executed. You can also get cocktails made from other spirits if gin isn't your thing. (📞06 6880 2452; www.facebook.com/thegincorner; Via Pallacorda 2, Hotel Adriano; ⏰6pm-midnight; 🚌Via di Monte Brianzo)

Entertainment

Teatro Argentina   THEATRE

24 ⭐ Map p42, C5

Founded in 1732, Rome's top theatre is one of the two official homes of the Teatro di Roma – the other is the **Teatro India** (✆06 68400 0311; www.teatrodiroma.net; Lungotevere Vittorio Gassman 1; Ⓜ️Stazione Trastevere) in the southern suburbs. Rossini's *Barber of Seville* premiered here in 1816 and it today stages a wide-ranging program of drama (mostly in Italian), high-profile dance performances and classical music concerts. (✆06 68400 0311; www.teatrodiroma.net; Largo di Torre Argentina 52; tickets €12-32; 🚃Largo di Torre Argentina)

Shopping

Confetteria Moriondo & Gariglio   CHOCOLATE

25 🔒 Map p42, D4

Roman poet Trilussa was so smitten with this historic chocolate shop – established by the Torinese confectioners to the royal house of Savoy – that he was moved to mention it in verse. And we agree, it's a gem. Decorated like an elegant tearoom, with crimson walls, tables and glass cabinets, it specialises in delicious handmade chocolates, many prepared according to original 19th-century recipes. (✆06 699 0856; Via del Piè di Marmo 21-22; ⏰9am-7.30pm Mon-Sat; 🚃Via del Corso)

Ibiz – Artigianato in Cuoio   FASHION & ACCESSORIES

26 🔒 Map p42, B6

In her diminutive family workshop, Elisa Nepi and her team craft exquisite, soft-as-butter leather wallets, bags, belts and sandals, in simple but classy designs and myriad colours. You can pick up a belt for about €35, while for a bag you should bank on at least €110. (✆06 6830 7297; www.ibizroma.it; Via dei Chiavari 39; ⏰9.30am-7.30pm Mon-Sat; 🚃Corso Vittorio Emanuele II)

🔍 Local Life
Il Campo

Noisy, colourful **Campo de' Fiori** (Map p42, B5; 🚃Corso Vittorio Emanuele II) is a major focus of Roman life: by day it hosts one of Rome's best-known **markets** (⏰7am-2pm Mon-Sat), while at night it morphs into a raucous open-air pub as drinkers spill out from its many bars and eateries. For centuries the square was the site of public executions, and it was here that philosopher Giordano Bruno was burned for heresy in 1600. The spot is marked by a sinister statue of the hooded monk, which was created by Ettore Ferrari in 1889.

Marta Ray SHOES

27 Map p42, A2

Women's ballet flats and elegant, everyday bags, in rainbow colours and butter-soft leather, are the hallmarks of the emerging Marta Ray brand. At this store, one of three in town, you'll find a selection of trademark ballerinas and a colourful line in modern, beautifully designed handbags. (06 6880 2641; www.martaray.it; Via dei Coronari 121; 10am-8pm; Via Zanardelli)

Bartolucci TOYS

28 Map p42, D3

It's difficult to resist going into this magical toyshop where everything is carved out of wood. By the main entrance, a Pinocchio pedals his bike robotically, perhaps dreaming of the full-size motorbike parked nearby, while inside there are all manner of ticking clocks, rocking horses, planes and more Pinocchios than you're likely to see in your whole life. (www. bartolucci.com; Via dei Pastini 98; 10am-10.30pm; Via del Corso)

Salumeria Roscioli FOOD & DRINKS

29 Map p42, B6

The rich scents of cured meats, cheeses, conserves, olive oil and balsamic vinegar intermingle at this top-class deli, one of Rome's finest. Alongside iconic Italian products, you'll also find a vast choice of wines and a range of French cheeses, Spanish hams and Scottish salmon. (06 687 5287; www. salumeriaroscioli.com; Via dei Giubbonari 21; 8.30am-8.30pm Mon-Sat; Via Arenula)

namasTèy TEA

30 Map p42, C4

After a visit to this charming shop, you'll be reminded of it every time you have a tea. Set up like an apothecary with ceiling-high shelves and rows of jars, it stocks blends from across the globe, as well as everything you could ever need for your home tea ritual – teapots, cups, infusers and filters. It also sells coffee and bite-size snacks. (06 6813 5660; www.namastey.it; Via della Palombella 26; 10.30am-7.30pm Tue-Sat, 11.30am-7.30pm Sun, closed Aug; Largo di Torre Argentina)

Understand
Architectural Timeline

c 4th century BC–AD 5th century The ancient Romans make huge advances in engineering techniques, constructing monumental public buildings, bridges, aqueducts, housing blocks and an underground sewerage system.

4th–12th centuries Church building is the focus of architectural activity in the Middle Ages as Rome's early Christian leaders seek to stamp their authority on the city.

15th–16th centuries Based on humanism and a reappraisal of classical precepts, the Renaissance hits an all-time high in the first two decades of the 16th century, a period known as the High Renaissance.

17th century Developing out of the Counter-Reformation, the baroque flourishes in Rome, fuelled by Church money and the genius of Gian Lorenzo Bernini and his hated rival Francesco Borromini.

18th century A short-lived but theatrical style born out of the baroque, the florid rococo gifts Rome some of its most popular sights.

late 18th–19th centuries Piazza del Popolo takes on its current form and Villa Torlonia gets a facelift courtesy of Rome's top neoclassical architect, Giuseppe Valadier.

late 19th century Rome gets a major post-unification makeover – roads are built, piazzas are laid, and residential quarters spring up to house government bureaucrats.

early 20th century Muscular and modern, Italian rationalism plays to Mussolini's vision of a fearless, futuristic Rome, a 20th-century *caput mundi* (world capital).

1990s–present Rome provides the historic stage upon which some of the world's top contemporary architects experiment. Criticism and praise are meted out in almost equal measure.

Explore

Tridente

This central part of Rome is glamorous, debonair and tourist-busy. Designer boutiques, fashionable bars, swish hotels and a handful of historic cafes and trattorias lace the compelling web of streets between Piazza di Spagna and Piazza del Popolo.

The Sights in a Day

Breakfast at **Antico Caffè Greco** (p62), the one-time refuge of Romantic poets, before heading up to **Piazza di Spagna and the Spanish Steps** (p56). Climb the staircase to the **Chiesa della Trinità dei Monti** (p57) where you'll be rewarded with wonderful rooftop views. While you're here, visit the **Pincio Hill Gardens** (p60) and **Villa Medici** (p60).

Head back down the stairs to sample the pasta at **Pastificio** (p61). Next, search out **Via Margutta** (p61), the charming street that was once home to Federico Fellini. Follow on to the grand **Piazza del Popolo** (p59) and the art-rich **Basilica di Santa Maria del Popolo** (p59). Make your way to the **Museo dell'Ara Pacis** (p60) to admire ancient stonework. Afterwards, indulge in some retail therapy in the stores and boutiques on Via del Corso, **Via dei Condotti** (p64; pictured left) and Via del Babuino, stopping for a pick-me-up at tiramisu vendor **Pompi** (p62).

Start the evening with a drink at **Il Palazzetto** (p62) before dinner at **Fiaschetteria Beltramme** (p60). Round the day off with some celeb-watching over cocktails at the **Stravinskij Bar** (p64).

⊙ Top Sight

Spanish Steps & Piazza di Spagna (p56)

♥ Best of Rome

History
Basilica di Santa Maria del Popolo (p59)

Food
Imàgo (p61)

Fatamorgana Corso (p62)

Bars & Nightlife
Zuma Bar (p63)

Architecture
Museo dell'Ara Pacis (p60)

Shopping
Re(f)use (p64)

Gente (p64)

Manila Grace (p65)

Getting There

Ⓜ Metro Spagna and Flaminio stations are perfectly placed for Tridente. Both stops are on line A.

🚌 Bus Numerous buses stop at the southern end of Via del Corso and on Via del Tritone, ideal for a foray into Tridente.

Top Sights
Spanish Steps & Piazza di Spagna

A magnet for visitors since the 18th century, the Spanish Steps (Scalinata della Trinità dei Monti) rising up from Piazza di Spagna provide a perfect people-watching perch: think hot spot for selfies, newly-wed couples posing for romantic photos etc. In the late 1700s the area was much loved by English visitors on the Grand Tour and was known to locals as the *ghetto de l'inglesi* (the English ghetto).

👁 Map p58, D4

Ⓜ Spagna

Spanish Steps, with the Fontana della Barcaccia in the foreground

The Spanish Steps

Piazza di Spagna was named after the Spanish Embassy to the Holy See, but the staircase – 135 gleaming steps designed by the Italian Francesco de Sanctis and built in 1725 with a legacy from the French – leads up to the hilltop French Chiesa della Trinità dei Monti. The dazzling sweep of stairs reopened in September 2016 after a €1.5 million clean-up job funded by luxury Italian jewellery house Bulgari.

Keats-Shelley House

At the foot of the Spanish Steps, this **house-museum** (☐06 678 42 35; www.keats-shelley-house.org; Piazza di Spagna 26; adult/reduced €5/4; ⊙10am-1pm & 2-6pm Mon-Sat; ⓂSpagna) is where Romantic poet John Keats died of TB at the age of 25, in February 1821. Keats came to Rome in 1820 to try to improve his health in the Italian climate, and rented two rooms on the 3rd floor of a townhouse next to the Spanish Steps, with painter companion Joseph Severn (1793–1879).

Chiesa della Trinità dei Monti

This landmark **church** (Map p58; ☐06 679 41 79; Piazza Trinità dei Monti 3; ⊙7.30am-8pm Tue-Fri, 10am-5pm Sat & Sun; ⓂSpagna) was commissioned by King Louis XII of France and consecrated in 1585. Apart from the great city views from its front steps, it has some wonderful frescoes by Daniele da Volterra. His *Deposizione* (Deposition), in the second chapel on the left, is regarded as a masterpiece of mannerist painting.

Fontana della Barcaccia

At the foot of the steps, the fountain of a sinking boat, the Barcaccia (1627), is believed to be by Pietro Bernini, father of the more famous Gian Lorenzo. It's fed from the ancient Roman Acqua Vergine aqueduct. Here there's not much pressure, so it's sunken as a clever piece of engineering.

☑ Top Tips

▶ No picnics on the steps, please! It is forbidden to eat and drink or 'shout, squall and sing' on the beautifully restored staircase. Doing so risks a fine of €25 to €500.

▶ A prime photo op is during the springtime festival Mostra delle Azalee, held late March/early April, when hundreds of vases of bright pink azaleas in bloom adorn the steps.

▶ To skip the 135-step hike up, take the lift inside the Spagna metro station to the top.

✗ Take a Break

Play the Grand Tour tourist with afternoon tea at 19th-century Babington's Tea Rooms (p64), at the foot of the Spanish Steps.

Watch the sun set over the steps from the fabulous ringside terrace of cocktail bar Il Palazzetto (p62).

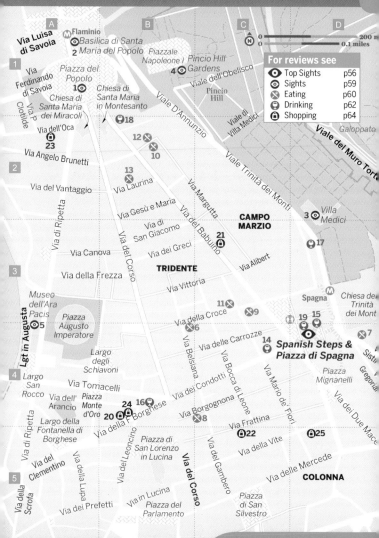

Via Luisa di Savoia

Ⓜ Flaminio

◉ Basilica di Santa
2 Maria del Popolo

Via Ferdinando di Savoia

Piazza del Popolo
1 ◉

Via P Clotilde

Chiesa di Santa Maria dei Miracoli

Chiesa di Santa Maria in Montesanto

Via dell'Oca
23 🛍

Via Angelo Brunetti

Piazzale Napoleone I

Pincio Hill

4 ◉ Gardens

Viale dell'Obelisco

Pincio Hill

Viale di Villa Medici

Galoppato

Viale del Muro Tort

For reviews see
◉ Top Sights   p56
◉ Sights   p59
🍴 Eating   p60
🍷 Drinking   p62
🛍 Shopping   p64

Viale D'Annunzio

18 🍴

12 ✕
10

Via del Vantaggio

13
Via Laurina

Via Gesù e Maria

Via di Ripetta

Via di San Giacomo

Via Margutta

Via del Babuino

21 🛍

Viale Trinità dei Monti

CAMPO MARZIO

3 ◉ Villa Medici

17

Via Canova

Via dei Greci

Via Alibert

Via della Frezza

TRIDENTE

Via Vittoria

Spagna **Ⓜ**

Chiesa de Trinità dei Mont

Museo dell'Ara Pacis
5 ◉

Piazza Augusto Imperatore

11 ✕
Via della Croce
6 🍴

✕ 9

19 15
🍷 🛍

7

Lgt in Augusta

Largo degli Schiavoni

Via delle Carrozze

14 🛍

Spanish Steps & Piazza di Spagna

Sisti

Largo San Rocco

Via Tomacelli

Via dell' Arancio

Piazza Monte d'Oro

24 16 🍴
20 🛍

Via della F Borghese

Via Belsiana

Via dei Condotti

Via Bocca di Leone

Via dei Condotti

Via Borgognona

✕ 8

Via Mario de' Fiori

Piazza Mignanelli

Gregori

Via dei Due Mace

Largo della Fontanella di Borghese

Via del Clementino

Via di Ripetta

Via del Leoncino

Via della Lupa

Piazza di San Lorenzo in Lucina

Via del Corso

Via Frattina

22 🛍

25 🛍

Via della Vite

Via delle Mercede

COLONNA

Via della Scrofa

Via in Lucina

Via dei Prefetti

Piazza del Parlamento

Via del Gambero

Piazza di San Silvestro

200 m
0.1 miles

Piazza del Popolo

Sights

Piazza del Popolo   PIAZZA

1 ⊙ Map p58, A1

This dazzling piazza was laid out in 1538 to provide a grandiose entrance to what was then Rome's main northern gateway. It has since been remodelled several times, most recently by Giuseppe Valadier in 1823. Guarding its southern approach are Carlo Rainaldi's twin 17th-century churches, **Chiesa di Santa Maria dei Miracoli** (Map p58; Via del Corso 528; ⊗6.45am-12.30pm & 4.30-7.30pm Mon-Sat, 8am-1.15pm & 4.30-7.45 Sun) and **Chiesa di Santa Maria in Montesanto** (Chiesa degli Artisti; Map p58; www.chiesadegliartisti.it; Via del Babuino 198; ⊗5.30-8pm Mon-Fri, 11am-1.30pm Sun). In the centre, the 36m-high obelisk was brought by Augustus from ancient Egypt; it originally stood in Circo Massimo. (Ⓜ Flaminio)

Basilica di Santa Maria del Popolo   BASILICA

2 ⊙ Map p58, A1

A magnificent repository of art, this is one of Rome's earliest and richest Renaissance churches. Of the numerous works of art on display, it is the two Caravaggio masterpieces that draw the most onlookers – the *Conversion of Saul* (1601) and the *Crucifixion of St Peter* (1601), in a chapel to the left of the main altar – but it contains other fine works, including several by Pinturicchio and Bernini. (www.smariadelpopolo.com; Piazza del Popolo 12; ⏱10.30am-12.30pm & 4-6.30pm Mon-Thu, 10.30am-6.30pm Fri & Sat, 4.30-6.30pm Sun; Ⓜ Flaminio)

Villa Medici
PALACE

3 ◉ Map p58, D2

This sumptuous Renaissance palace was built for Cardinal Ricci da Montepulciano in 1540, but Ferdinando dei Medici bought it in 1576. It remained in Medici hands until 1801, when Napoleon acquired it for the French Academy. Guided tours take in the wonderful landscaped gardens, cardinal's painted apartments, and incredible views over Rome – tours in English depart at noon. Note the pieces of ancient Roman sculpture from the Ara Pacis embedded in the villa's walls. (☎06 676 13 11; www.villamedici.it; Viale Trinità dei Monti 1; 1½hr guided tour adult/reduced €12/6; ⏱10am-7pm Tue-Sun; Ⓜ Spagna)

Pincio Hill Gardens
GARDENS

4 ◉ Map p58, B1

Overlooking Piazza del Popolo, 19th-century Pincio Hill is named after the Pinci family, who owned this part of Rome in the 4th century. It's quite a climb up from the piazza, but at the top you're rewarded with lovely views over to St Peter's and the Gianicolo Hill. Alternatively, approach from the top of the Spanish Steps. From the gardens, strike out to explore Villa Borghese, Villa Medici or Chiesa della

Trinità dei Monti (p57) at the top of the Spanish Steps. (Ⓜ Flaminio)

Museo dell'Ara Pacis
MUSEUM

5 ◉ Map p58, A4

The first modern construction in Rome's historic centre since WWII, Richard Meier's controversial and widely detested glass-and-marble pavilion houses the *Ara Pacis Augustae* (Altar of Peace), Augustus' great monument to peace. One of the most important works of ancient Roman sculpture, the vast marble altar – measuring 11.6m by 10.6m by 3.6m – was completed in 13 BC. (☎06 06 08; www.arapacis.it; Lungotevere in Auga; adult/reduced €11/9; ⏱9.30am-7.30pm Mon-Sat; Ⓜ Flaminio)

Eating

Fiaschetteria Beltramme
TRATTORIA €€

6 ✗ Map p58, B4

A super spot for authentic Roman dining near the Spanish Steps, Fiaschetteria (meaning 'wine-sellers') is a hole-in-the-wall, stuck-in-time place with a short menu. Fashionistas with appetites dig into traditional Roman dishes made using recipes unchanged since the 1930s when a waiter at the 19th-century wine bar (from 1886 to be precise) started serving food. Seeking the perfect carbonara? This is the address. (☎06 6979 7200; Via della Croce 39; meals €40; ⏱12.15-3pm & 7.30-10.45pm; Ⓜ Spagna)

Imàgo

ITALIAN €€€

7 🍴 Map p58, D4

Even in a city of great views, the panoramas from the Hassler Hotel's Michelin-starred romantic rooftop restaurant are special, extending over a sea of roofs to the great dome of St Peter's Basilica; request the corner table. Complementing the views are the bold, mod-Italian creations of culinary whizz, chef Francesco Apreda. (☎ 06 6993 4726; www.imagorestaurant.com; Piazza della Trinità dei Monti 6, Hotel Hassler; tasting menus €120-150; ⊙ 7-10.30pm Feb-Dec; 🅿; Ⓜ Spagna)

Ginger

BRASSERIE €€

8 🍴 Map p58, C4

This buzzy white-tiled space is a fantastic all-day dining spot near the Spanish Steps. The focus is on organic 'slow food' dishes using seasonal AOP ingredients, and all appetites are catered for with gourmet, French baguette-style sandwiches, steamed 'baskets', meal-sized salads and healthy mains like salmon with orange mayonnaise. (☎ 06 9603 6390; www.ginger.roma.it; Via Borgognona 43; sandwiches €7-10, salads €9-14, meals €50; ⊙ 10am-11.30pm; Ⓜ Spagna)

Pastificio

FAST FOOD €

9 🍴 Map p58, C3

A brilliant budget find, this old-fashioned pasta shop (1918) with kitchen hatch serves up two choices of pasta at lunchtime. It's fast food, Italian style – freshly cooked (if you time it right) pasta, with wine and water included. Grab a space to stand and eat between shelves packed with packets of dry pasta or take it away. (Via della Croce 8; pasta, wine & water €4; ⊙ 1-3pm Mon-Sat; Ⓜ Spagna)

Il Margutta

VEGETARIAN €€

10 🍴 Map p58, B2

This chic art-gallery-bar-restaurant gets packed at lunchtime with Romans feasting on its good-value, eat-as-much-as-you-can buffet deal. Everything is organic, with an evening menu tempting with creative dishes such as tofu with marinated ginger and smoked tubers, or grilled chicory with almond cream, almond cream

🔍 Local Life
Via Margutta

Small independent antique shops, art galleries and boutiques pepper **Via Margutta** (Map p58, C2; Ⓜ Spagna), one of Rome's prettiest pedestrian cobbled lanes strung with ivy-laced palazzi, decorative potted plants and the odd monumental fountain. The street is named after a 16th-century family of barbers but has long been associated with art and artists – Picasso worked at a gallery at No 54 and the Italian Futurists had their first meeting here in 1917. Audrey Hepburn and Gregory Peck also whispered sweet nothings to each other at No 51 in the classic *Roman Holiday* (1953).

and candied tangerine. Among the various tasting menus is a vegan option. (📞06 3265 0577; www.ilmargutta. bio; Via Margutta 118; lunch buffet weekdays/weekends €15/25, meals €15-40; ⏱8.30am-11.30pm; 🍴; Ⓜ Spagna, Flaminio)

Pompi   DESSERTS €

11 ✕ Map p58, C3

Rome's most famous vendor of tiramisu (which literally means 'pick me up') sells takeaway cartons of the deliciously yolky yet light-as-air dessert. As well as classic, it comes in pistachio, strawberry, hazelnut and banana-chocolate variations. Eat on the spot (standing) or buy frozen portions that will keep for a few hours until you're ready to tuck in at home. (www.barpompi.it; Via della Croce 82; tiramisu €4; ⏱10.30am-9.30pm; Ⓜ Spagna)

Babette   ITALIAN €€€

12 ✕ Map p58, B2

Babette is run by two sisters who used to produce a fashion magazine, hence the effortlessly chic interior of exposed brick walls and vintage painted signs. Cuisine is a feast of Italian dishes with a creative French twist: *tortiglioni* with courgette, saffron and pistachio pesto, for example, followed by rabbit loin in juniper sauce, then *torta Babette* (a light-as-air lemon cheesecake). (📞06 321 15 59; www.babette ristorante.it; Via Margutta 1d; meals €50; ⏱1-3pm & 7-10.45pm Tue-Sun, closed Jan; 🍴; Ⓜ Spagna, Flaminio)

Fatamorgana Corso   GELATO €

13 ✕ Map p58, B2

The wonderful all-natural, gluten-free gelato served at Fatamorgana is arguably Rome's best artisanal ice cream. Innovative and classic tastes of heaven abound, including flavours such as pear and caramel, all made from the finest seasonal ingredients. There are several branches around town. (📞06 3265 2238; www.gelateriafatamorgana.com; Via Laurina 10; 2/3/4/5 scoops €2.50/3.50/4.50/5; ⏱noon-11pm; Ⓜ Flaminio)

Drinking

Antico Caffè Greco   CAFE

14 ☕ Map p58, C4

Rome's oldest cafe, open since 1760, is still working the look with the utmost elegance: waiters in black tails and bow tie, waitresses in frilly white pinnies, scarlet flock walls and age-spotted gilt mirrors. Prices reflect this amazing heritage: pay €9 for a cappuccino sitting down or join locals for the same (€2.50) standing at the bar. (📞06 679 17 00; Via dei Condotti 86; ⏱9am-9pm; Ⓜ Spagna)

Il Palazzetto   CAFE, COCKTAIL BAR

15 ☕ Map p58, D3

No terrace proffers such a fine view of the comings and goings on the Spanish Steps over an expertly shaken cocktail (€10–13). Ride the lift up from the discreet entrance on narrow Via dei Bottino or look for steps leading

Antico Caffè Greco

to the bar from the top of the steps. Given everything is alfresco, the bar is only open in warm, dry weather. (☑06 6993 41000; Viccolo del Bottino 8; ⊙noon-8.30pm Tue-Sun, closed in rain; Ⓜ Spagna)

Zuma Bar
COCKTAIL BAR

16 Ⓟ Map p58, B4

Dress up for a drink on the rooftop terrace of Palazzo Fendi of fashion-house fame – few cocktail bars in Rome are as sleek, hip or achingly sophisticated as this. City rooftop views are predictably fabulous; cocktails mix exciting flavours like shiso with juniper berries, elderflower and *prosecco;* and DJ sets spin Zuma playlists at weekends. (☑06 9926 6622; www.zumarestaurant.com; Via della Fontanella di Borghese 48, Palazzo Fendi;

⊙6pm-1am Sun-Thu, to 2am Fri & Sat; 🛜; 🚊Via del Corso)

Caffè Ciampini
CAFE

17 Ⓟ Map p58, D3

Hidden away a short walk from the top of the Spanish Steps towards the Pincio Hill Gardens, this graceful seasonal cafe has a vintage garden-party vibe, with green wooden latticework and orange trees framing its white-clothed tables. There are lovely views over the backstreets behind Spagna, and the *gelato* – particularly the *tartufo al cioccolato* (chocolate truffle) – is renowned. Serves food too. (☑06 678 56 78; www.caffeciampini.com; Viale Trinità dei Monti; ⊙8am-11pm Mar-Oct; Ⓜ Spagna)

Stravinskij Bar   BAR

18 🔊 Map p58, B2

Can't afford to stay at the celeb-magnet Hotel de Russie? Then splash out on a drink at its swish bar. There are sofas inside, but best is a drink in the sunny courtyard, with sun-shaded tables overlooked by terraced gardens. Impossibly romantic in the best dolce vita style, it's perfect for a pricey cocktail or beer accompanied by appropriately posh bar snacks. (☎06 3288 8874; Via del Babuino 9, Hotel de Russie; ⏰9am-1am; Ⓜ Flaminio)

Babington's Tea Rooms   CAFE

19 🔊 Map p58, D4

Founded in 1893, at a time when tea could only be bought in pharmacies, Babington's Tea Rooms were opened by two English women with the intention of serving up a decent cuppa to the hordes of English tourists in Rome. Traditional cream teas, scones, muffins, fruity teacakes, dainty finger sandwiches, fried breakfasts and other English culinary treats remain its unique selling point. (☎06 678 08 46; www.babingtons.com; Piazza di Spagna 23; ⏰10am-9.15pm; Ⓜ Spagna)

Shopping

Re(f)use   DESIGN

20 🔒 Map p58, B4

Fascinating to browse, this clever boutique showcases unique Carmina Campus pieces – primarily bags and jewellery – made from upcycled objects and recycled fabrics. The brand is the love child of Rome-born designer Ilaria Venturini Fendi (of *the* Fendi family), a passionate advocate of ethical fashion, who crafts contemporary bracelets from beer and soft drink cans, and bold bags from recycled materials. (☎06 6813 6975; www.carminacampus.com; Via della Fontanelle di Borghese 40; ⏰11am-7pm; 🚌 Via del Corso)

Gente   FASHION & ACCESSORIES

21 🔒 Map p58, C3

This multi-label boutique was the first in Rome to bring all the big-name luxury designers – Italian, French and otherwise – under one roof and its vast emporium-styled space remains an essential stop for every serious fashionista. Labels include Dolce & Gabbana, Prada, Alexander McQueen, Sergio Rossi and Missoni.

Ⓠ Local Life

Via dei Condotti

High-rolling shoppers and window-dreamers will want to stroll **Via dei Condotti** (Map p58, B4; Ⓜ Spagna), Rome's smartest shopping strip. At the eastern end, Caffè Greco (p62) was a favourite meeting point of 18th- and 19th-century writers. Other top shopping streets in the area include Via Frattina, Via della Croce, Via delle Carrozze and Via del Babuino.

It has a sparkling new store for women at **Via Frattini** (☏06 678 91 32; Via Frattini 93; ⓤVia del Corso). (☏06 320 7671; www.genteroma.com; Via del Babuino 77; ⏱10.30am-7.30pm Mon-Thu, to 8pm Fri & Sat, 11.30am-7.30pm Sun; ⓜSpagna)

Manila Grace FASHION & ACCESSORIES

22 🔒 Map p58, C5

An essential homegrown label for dedicated followers of fashion, Manila Grace mixes bold prints, patterns and fabrics to create a strikingly unique, assertive style for women who like to stand out in a crowd. Think a pair of red stiletto shoes with a fuchsia-pink pom pom on the toe, a striped jacket or a glittering gold bag with traditional tan-leather trim. Alessia Santi is the talented designer behind the brand. (☏06 679 78 36; www.manilagrace.com; Via Frattina 60; ⏱10am-7.30pm; ⓜSpagna)

Artisanal Cornucopia DESIGN

23 🔒 Map p58, A2

One of several stylish independent boutiques on Via dell'Oca, this chic concept store showcases exclusive handmade pieces by Italian designers, such as a trunk full of Anthony Peto hats, bold sculpture-like lamps by Roman designer Vincenzo Del Pizzo, and delicate gold necklaces and other jewellery crafted by Giulia Barela. It also sells artisan bags, shoes, candles, homewares and other lovely hand-made objects. (☏342 871 4597; www.artisanalcornucopia.com; Via dell'Oca 38a; ⏱10am-7pm; ⓜFlaminio)

Flumen Profumi PERFUME

24 🔒 Map p58, B4

Unique 'made in Rome' scents is what this artisan perfumery on Tridente's smartest shopping strip is all about. Natural perfumes are oil-based, contain four to eight base notes and evoke *la dolce vita* in Italy. Incantro fuses pomegranate with white flower, while Ritrovarsi Ancora is a nostalgic fragrance evocative of long, lazy, family meals around a shared countryside table (you can smell the fig!). (☏06 6830 7635; www.flumenprofumi.com; Via della Fontanella di Borghese 41; ⏱11am-2pm & 3.30-8pm Mon-Sat, 11am-2pm & 3-7.30pm Sun; ⓤVia del Corso)

Anglo American Bookshop BOOKS

25 🔒 Map p58, D5

Particularly good for university reference books, the Anglo American Bookshop is well stocked and well known. It has an excellent range of literature, travel guides, children's books and maps, and if it hasn't got the book you want, it'll order it in. (☏06 679 52 22; www.aab.it; Via della Vite 102; ⏱3.30-7.30pm Mon, 10.30am-7.30pm Tue-Sat; ⓜSpagna)

Explore

Trevi & the Quirinale

The Roman hill of Quirinale is home to the extraordinary Trevi Fountain and the imposing Palazzo del Quirinale, as well as important churches by the twin masters of Roman baroque, Gian Lorenzo Bernini and Francesco Borromini. The area is also an artistic hot spot, with plenty of galleries. Lording over it all, the Palazzo del Quirinale exudes sober authority – and wonderful views of the Rome skyline at sunset.

The Sights in a Day

☼ Start the day with the majestic **Palazzo del Quirinale** (p71), then visit the vast private art collection in the **Galleria Colonna** (p71). Head to the **Trevi Fountain** (p68) to throw in your coin and ensure your return to Rome. By now, it's time for lunch at **Colline Emiliane** (p74).

☼ Fed and watered, prepare for plenty of baroque pomp and Renaissance revelations at **Palazzo Barberini** (p72), a superb art gallery housed in one of Rome's great aristo-cratic *palazzi* (mansions). Next visit Rome's strangest sight: crypt chapels made entirely of human bones in the **Convento dei Cappuccini** (p73). Shake off the macabre atmosphere with a drink at **Pepy's Bar** (p75).

☾ End your day with a Tuscan feast at **Vineria Il Chianti** (p74) followed by a whisky and music at **Gregory's Jazz Club** (p76).

◉ Top Sight
Trevi Fountain (p68)

♥ Best of Rome
History
Trevi Fountain (p68)

Food
Colline Emiliane (p74)

Culture
Gregory's Jazz Club (p76)

Getting There

Ⓜ **Metro** The Trevi and Quirinale areas are closest to the Barberini metro stop on line A.

🚌 **Bus** Numerous buses run down to Piazza Barberini or along Via Veneto.

Top Sights
Trevi Fountain

Rome's most famous fountain, the iconic Fontana di Trevi in Tridente, is a baroque extravaganza – a foaming white-marble and emerald-water masterpiece filling an entire piazza. The flamboyant baroque ensemble, 20m wide and 26m high, was designed by Nicola Salvi in 1732 and depicts seagod Oceanus's chariot being led by Tritons with seahorses – one wild, one docile – representing the moods of the sea.

◉ Map p70, B3

Piazza di Trevi

Ⓜ Barberini

Trevi Fountain is best at night: beautifully lit with quieter surrounds

Aqua Virgo

The fountain water comes from the Aqua Virgo, an underground aqueduct that is over 2000 years old, built by General Agrippa under Augustus and which brings water from the Salone springs around 19km away. The name Trevi refers to the *tre vie* (three roads) that converge at the fountain.

Salvi's Urn

To the eastern side of the fountain is a large round stone urn. The story goes that Salvi, during the construction of the fountain, was harassed by a barber, who had his shop to the east of the fountain and who was critical of the work in progress. Thus the sculptor added this urn in order to block this irritating critic.

Coin Tossing

The famous tradition (since the 1954 film *Three Coins in the Fountain)* is to toss a coin into the fountain, thus ensuring your return to Rome. Up to €3000 is thrown into the Trevi each day. This money is collected daily and goes to the Catholic charity Caritas, with its yield increasing significantly since the crackdown on people extracting the money for themselves.

Chiesa di Santissimi Vincezo e Anastasio

After tossing your lucky coin into Trevi Fountain, nip into this 17th-century **church** (www.santivincenzo eanastasio.it; Vicolo dei Modelli 73; ⏰9am-1pm & 4-8pm; Ⓜ Barberini) overlooking Rome's most spectacular fountain. Originally known as the 'Papal church' due to its proximity to the papal residence on Quirinal Hill, the church safeguards the hearts and internal organs of dozens of popes – preserved in amphorae in a tiny gated chapel to the right of the apse. This practice began under Pope Sixtus V (1585–90) and continued until the 20th century when Pope Pius X (1903–14) decided it was not for him.

☑ Top Tips

▶ Coin-tossing etiquette: throw with your right hand, over your left shoulder with your back facing the fountain.

▶ Paddling or bathing in the fountain is strictly forbidden, as is eating and drinking on the steps leading down to the water. Both crimes risk an on-the-spot fine of up to €500.

▶ The fountain gets very busy during the day; visit later in the evening when it's beautifully lit instead.

✖ Take a Break

San Crispino (☎06 679 39 24; www.ilgelatodisan crispino.com; Via della Panetteria 42; tubs around €2.50; ⏰11am-12.30am Sun-Thu, to 1.30am Fri & Sat; Ⓜ Barberini) is the nearest recommended *gelateria* for an ice to cool down with after admiring the fountain.

Authentic dining spots near the fountain include Vineria Il Chianti (p74) and Hostaria Romana (p74).

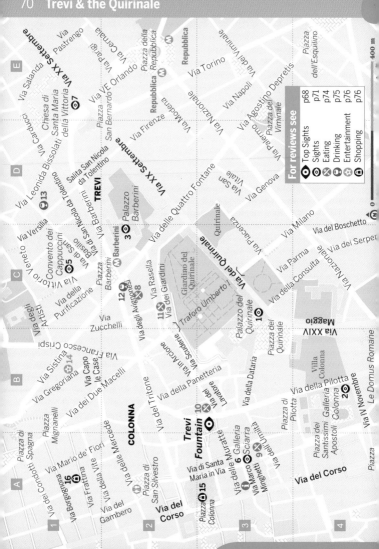

400 m

Piazza della Repubblica

Republica

Piazza dell'Esquilino

Via Pastrengo
Via Cernaia
Via Parigi
Via della Repubblica
Via del Viminale

Via XX Settembre

Via Salandra
Via Carducci
Chiesa di Santa Maria della Vittoria ◎7
Via VE Orlando
Piazza San Bernardo
Via Firenze
Via Modena
Via Torino
Via Napoli

Republica

Via Agostino Depretis
Piazza dei Viminale

Via Leonida Bissolati
Via XX Settembre
Salita San Nicola da Tolentino
Via Nazionale
Via Palermo

Via Versilia
Convento dei Cappuccini
TREVI
◎13
Via di San Nicola da Tolentino
Via di San Basilio
◎5
Via Barberini
◎3 Palazzo Barberini
Via delle Quattro Fontane
Via San Vitale
Via Genova

Via Vittorio Veneto
Via degli Artisti
Via della Purificazione
Piazza Barberini
Ⓜ Barberini
Via Rasella
Via Zucchelli
◎12 ⊗8
Via degli Avignonesi
Giardino del Quirinale
Quirinale
Via Piacenza
Via della Consulta
Via Parma
Via Milano
Via del Boschetto
Via dei Serpen...

Via Sistina
Via Gregoriana
⊗14
Piazza Mignanelli
Via Francesco Crispi
⊗11
Via degli Avignonesi
Traforo Umberto I
Palazzo del Quirinale
◎1
Via Nazionale

Piazza di Spagna
Via Capo le Case
Via dei Due Macelli
Via del Tritone
Via in Arcione
Via delle Scuderie
Piazza del Quirinale

COLONNA
Via della Panetteria
Via della Dataria
Via XXIV Maggio
Villa Colonna

Via Borgognona
◉16
Via Mario de' Fiori
Via Frattina
Via della Vite
Via delle Mercede
Piazza di San Silvestro
Laverde
Vaccaro
◉10
Trevi Fountain ◉
Via della Murate
⊗6 ⊗ Galleria
Via Marco Sciarra
⊗9
Via dell'Unità
Via della Pilotta
Galleria Colonna
Le Domus Romane

Piazza di Spagna
Via del Gambero
Via del Corso
Piazza ◉15 Colonna
Via di Santa Maria in Via
Via Minghetti
Piazza di Pilotta
Piazza dei Santissimi Apostoli
Colonna
Piazza

Via del Corso

DANILO ASCIONE/SHUTTERSTOCK ©

Palazzo del Quirinale

Sights

Palazzo del Quirinale   PALACE

1 ◎ Map p70, C3

Overlooking Piazza del Quirinale, this immense palace is the official residence of Italy's head of state, the President of the Republic. For almost three centuries it was the pope's summer residence, but in 1870 Pope Pius IX begrudgingly handed the keys over to Italy's new king. Later, in 1948, it was given to the Italian state. Visits, by guided tour only, should be booked at least five days ahead by telephone (collect tour tickets at the nearby Infopoint at Salita di Montecavallo 15)

or buy online at www.coopculture.it. (✆ 06 3996 7557; www.quirinale.it; Piazza del Quirinale; 1¼hr tour €1.50, 2½hr tour adult/reduced €10/5; ⊙ 9.30am-4pm Tue, Wed & Fri-Sun, closed Aug; MBarberini)

Galleria Colonna   GALLERY

2 ◎ Map p70, B4

The only part of Palazzo Colonna open to the public, this opulent 17th-century gallery houses the Colonna family's private art collection. It's not the capital's largest collection but with works by Salvatore Rosa, Guido Reni, Guercino and Annibale Carracci, it's well worth the ticket price, which includes an optional guided tour in

English at noon. (✆ 06 678 43 50; www.galleriacolonna.it; Via della Pilotta 17; adult/reduced €12/10; ⏱ 9am-1.15pm Sat, closed Aug; 🚊 Via IV Novembre)

Palazzo Barberini
GALLERY

3 ◎ Map p70, C2

Commissioned to celebrate the Barberini family's rise to papal power, Palazzo Barberini is a sumptuous baroque palace that impresses even before you clap eyes on the breathtaking art. Many high-profile architects worked on it, including rivals Bernini and Borromini; the former contributed a large squared staircase, the latter a helicoidal one. Amid the masterpieces, don't miss Pietro da Cortona's *Il Trionfo della Divina Provvidenza* (Triumph of Divine Providence; 1632–39), the most spectacular of the *palazzo*

ceiling frescoes in the 1st-floor main salon. (Galleria Nazionale d'Arte Antica; ✆ 06 481 45 91; www.barberinicorsini.org; Via delle Quattro Fontane 13; adult/reduced €5/2.50, incl Palazzo Corsini €10/5; ⏱ 8.30am-7pm Tue-Sun; Ⓜ Barberini)

Le Domus Romane di Palazzo Valentini
ARCHAEOLOGICAL SITE

4 ◎ Map p70, B4

Underneath a grand mansion that's been the seat of the Province of Rome since 1873 lie the archaeological remains of several lavish ancient Roman houses; the excavated fragments have been turned into a fascinating multimedia 'experience'. Tours are every 30 minutes, but alternate between Italian, English and French. Book ahead online

---

Understand
Miraculous Madonnas

Overlooking Vicolo delle Bollette, a tiny lane near the Trevi Fountain, there's a small, simple painting of the Virgin Mary. This is the *Madonna della Pietà*, one of the most famous of Rome's *madonnelle* (small madonnas). There are estimated to be around 730 of these roadside madonnas in Rome's historic centre, most placed on street corners or outside historic *palazzi*. Many were added in the 16th and 17th centuries, but their origins date to pagan times when votive wall shrines were set up at street corners to honour the Lares, household spirits believed to protect passers-by. When Christianity emerged in the 4th century AD, these shrines were simply rededicated to the religion's new icons. Their presence was also intended to deter devout Catholics from committing street crime.

As well as food for the soul, the madonnas also provided a valuable public service. Until street lamps were introduced in the 19th century, the candles and lamps that lit up the images were the city's only source of street lighting.

or by phone, especially during holiday periods. (☏06 2276 1280; www.palazzo valentini.it; Via Foro Traiano 85; adult/reduced €12/8, advance booking fee €1.50; ⊙9.30am-6.30pm Wed-Mon; ♿; Ⓜ Barberini)

Convento dei Cappuccini
MUSEUM

5 ◉ Map p70, C1

This church and convent complex safeguards what is possibly Rome's strangest sight: crypt chapels where everything from the picture frames to the light fittings is made of human bones. Between 1732 and 1775 resident Capuchin monks used the bones of 3700 of their departed brothers to create this macabre *memento mori* (reminder of death) – a 30m-long passageway ensnaring six crypts, each named after the type of bone used to decorate, such as skulls, shin bones, pelvises etc. (☏06 487 11 85; www.cappucciniviaveneto.it; Via Vittorio Veneto 27; adult/reduced €8.50/5; ⊙9am-7pm; Ⓜ Barberini)

Galleria Sciarra
MONUMENT

6 ◉ Map p70, A3

Meander west from Trevi Fountain, along pedestrian Via delle Muratte, and duck a block south to this magnificent Art Nouveau courtyard, hidden away on Via Marco Minghetti. Part of 16th-century Palazzo Sciarra Colonna di Carbognano, both frescoes and iron-and-glass roof date to 1890 when the courtyard was remodelled

and spruced up by the wealthy Sciarra family. Admire the female virtues of strength, patience, modesty and kindness alongside aristocratic Roman women in their traditional roles as wife, mother, musician and so on. (Via Marco Minghetti 9-10; ⊙9am-8pm Mon-Fri; Ⓜ Barberini)

Chiesa di Santa Maria della Vittoria
CHURCH

7 ◉ Map p70, E1

This modest church is an unlikely setting for an extraordinary work of art – Bernini's extravagant and sexually charged *Santa Teresa trafitta dall'amore di Dio* (Ecstasy of St Teresa). This daring sculpture depicts Teresa, engulfed in the folds of a flowing cloak, floating in ecstasy on a cloud while a teasing angel pierces her repeatedly with a golden arrow. (☏06 4274 0571; Via XX Settembre 17; ⊙8.30am-noon & 3.30-6pm; Ⓜ Repubblica)

Local Life

Un Caffè

Prendere un caffè (having a coffee) is one of the great rituals of Roman life. As a rule, locals will stop at a bar for a coffee in the morning before work, and then again after lunch. To fit in with the crowd, ask for *un caffè* (the term *espresso* is rarely used) and drink standing at the bar. Also, never order a cappuccino after lunch.

Eating

Colline Emiliane   ITALIAN €€€

8   Map p70, C2

Sensational regional cuisine from Emilia-Romagna aside, what makes this small white-tablecloth dining address so outstanding is its family vibe and overwhelmingly warm service. It's been a stronghold of the Latini family since the 1930s, and today son Luca runs the show with his mother Paola (dessert queen), aunt Anna (watch her making fresh pasta each morning in the glassed-off lab) and father Massimo. (☑06 481 75 38; www.collineemiliane. com; Via degli Avignonesi 22; meals €45; ⏱12.45-2.45pm & 7.30-10.45pm Tue-Sun, closed Sun dinner & Mon; Ⓜ Barberini)

Bistro del Quirino   ITALIAN €

9   Map p70, A3

For unbeatable value near Trevi Fountain, reserve a table at this artsy bistro adjoining Teatro Quirino. Theatre posters add bags of colour to the spacious interior where a banquet of a self-service 'brunch' buffet – fantastic salads, antipasti, hot and cold dishes – is laid out for knowing Romans to feast on. (☑06 9887 8090; www.bistrotquirino.com; Via delle Vergini 7; brunch €10, à la carte €25; ⏱noon-3.30pm & 4pm-2am; Ⓠ Via del Corso)

Vineria Il Chianti   TUSCAN €€

10   Map p70, B3

With a name like Il Chianti, this pretty ivy-clad wine bar can only be Tuscan. Cosy up inside its bottle-lined interior or grab a table on the street terrace and dig into superb Tuscan dishes like *stracotto al Brunello* (beef braised in Brunello wine) or handmade pasta laced with *lardo di Colonnata* (aromatic pork fat aged in Carrara marble vats). (☑06 679 24 70; www.vineriailchianti. com; Via del Lavatore 81-82a; meals €45; ⏱10am-1am; Ⓠ Via del Tritone)

Hostaria Romana   TRATTORIA €€

11   Map p70, C2

A highly recommended address for lunch or dinner near Trevi Fountain, Hostaria Romana cooks up meaty, traditional classics like grilled goat chops, veal cutlets, roast suckling pig and T-bone steaks to a mixed Roman and tourist crowd. Busy, bustling and noisy, this is everything an Italian *trattoria* should be. Sign your name on the graffiti-covered walls before leaving. (☑06 474 52 84; www. hostariaromana.it; Via del Boccaccio 1; meals €40; ⏱12.30-3pm & 7.15-11pm Mon-Sat; Ⓜ Barberini)

Penne with tomato sauce and parmesan cheese

Drinking

Pepy's Bar
CAFE

12 🍷 Map p70, C2

Play the Roman: sit at a bistro table on the narrow pavement terrace and watch the fountains gush and *motorini* whizz by on Piazza Barberini at this down-to-earth, neighbourhood cafe in Trevi. It is a perfect spot for a relaxed drink any time of day, and its all-day sandwiches – made with perfectly square, crustless white bread – are almost too beautiful to eat. (🕿06 4040 2364; www.pepysbar.it; Piazza Barberini 53; ⏰7am-2am; 🛜; Ⓜ Barberini)

Moma
CAFE

13 🍷 Map p70, D1

Molto trendy: this cafe-restaurant is a find. It's sleekly sexy and popular with workers in suits from nearby offices. There's a small stand-up cafe downstairs, with a nice little deck outside where you can linger longer over coffee and delicious *dolcetti*. Upstairs is a recommended *cucina creativa* (creative cuisine) restaurant. (🕿06 4201 1798; www.ristorantemoma.it; Via di San Basilio 42; tasting menu €55 ⏰8am-midnight Mon-Sat Sep-Jul; Ⓜ Barberini)

Entertainment

Gregory's Jazz Club JAZZ

14 ⭐ Map p70, B1

If Gregory's were a tone of voice, it'd be husky: unwind over a whisky in the downstairs bar, then unwind some more on squashy sofas upstairs to slinky live jazz and swing, with quality local performers who also like to hang out here. (📞06 679 63 86; www.gregorys jazz.com; Via Gregoriana 54d; obligatory drink €15-20; ⏰8pm-2am Tue-Sun; Ⓜ Barberini, Spagna)

Shopping

Galleria Alberto Sordi SHOPPING CENTRE

15 🔒 Map p70, A3

This elegant stained-glass arcade appeared in Alberto Sordi's 1973 classic, *Polvere di stelle* (Stardust), and has since been renamed for Rome's favourite actor, who died in 2003. It's a serene place to browse stores such as Zara and Feltrinelli, and there's an airy cafe ideal for a quick coffee break. (📞06 6919 0769; www.galleriaalbertosordi. it; Piazza Colonna, Galleria di Piazza Colonna; ⏰8.30am-9pm Mon-Sat, 9.30am-9pm Sun; 🚌Via del Corso)

Fausto Santini SHOES

16 🔒 Map p70, A1

Rome's best-known shoe designer, Fausto Santini, is famous for his beguilingly simple, architectural shoe designs, with beautiful boots and shoes made from butter-soft leather. Colours are beautiful, and the quality, impeccable. Seek out the end-of-line **discount shop** (📞06 488 09 34; Via Cavour 106; ⏰10am-1pm & 3.30-7.30pm Tue-Fri, 10am-1pm & 3-7.30pm Sat; Ⓜ Cavour) if the shoes here are out of your price range. (📞06 678 41 14; www.faustosantini.com; Via Frattina 120; ⏰11am-7.30pm Mon-Sat, to 7pm Sun; Ⓜ Spagna)

Understand

Rome on Film

The Golden Age

For the golden age of Roman film-making you have to turn the clocks back to the 1940s, when Roberto Rossellini (1906–77) produced a trio of neorealist masterpieces. The first and most famous was *Roma città aperta* (Rome Open City; 1945), filmed with brutal honesty in the Prenestina district east of the city centre. Vittorio de Sica (1901–74) kept the neorealist ball rolling in 1948 with *Ladri di biciclette* (Bicycle Thieves), again filmed in Rome's sprawling suburbs.

Federico Fellini (1920–94) took the creative baton from the neorealists and carried it into the following decades. His disquieting style demands more of audiences, abandoning realistic shots for pointed images at once laden with humour, pathos and symbolism. Fellini's greatest international hit was *La Dolce Vita* (1960), starring Marcello Mastroianni and Anita Ekberg.

Contemporary Directors

Born in Naples but Roman by adoption, Paolo Sorrentino (b 1970) is the big name in Italian cinema. Since winning an Oscar for his 2013 hit *La grande bellezza* (The Great Beauty), he has gone on to direct Michael Caine and Harvey Keitel in *Youth* (2015) and Jude Law in the HBO–Atlantic Sky series *The Young Pope* (2016), a sumptuous, and at times surreal, tale of Vatican intrigue.

In contrast to Sorrentino, a Neapolitan best known for a film about Rome, Matteo Garrone (b 1968) is a Roman famous for a film about Naples. *Gomorra* (Gomorrah; 2008), his hard-hitting exposé of the Neapolitan *camorra* (mafia), enjoyed widespread acclaim.

More recently, Emanuele Crialese (b 1965) impressed with *Terraferma* (Dry Land; 2011), a thought-provoking study of immigration, and Lamberto Sanfelice won applause at the 2015 Sundance Film Festival for *Cloro* (Chlorine), a slow-burning drama centred on a teenage girl's struggles to keep her dreams alive in the face of family tragedy.

Local Life
San Lorenzo & Pigneto

Getting There

🚌 Take buses 7 and 492 for San Lorenzo; for Pigneto buses 81, 810, 105 and n12.

🚃 Catch tram 3 for San Lorenzo; tram 5, 14 or 19 for Pigneto.

A lively student quarter east of Termini, San Lorenzo is a metropolitan mix of graffiti-clad streets, artists studios, cheap takeaways and hip restaurants. Apart from a major basilica, there are few traditional sights, but come evening the area bursts into life. Southeast, the former working-class Pigneto district is one of the capital's coolest, a bar-heavy pocket frequented by bohemians, hipsters and trend-setting urbanites.

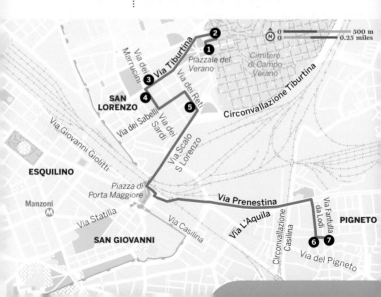

❶ Basilica di San Lorenzo Fuori le Mura

One of Rome's four patriarchal basilicas, the starkly beautiful **Basilica di San Lorenzo Fuori le Mura** (Piazzale San Lorenzo; ⊙8am-noon & 4-6.30pm; 🚃Piazzale del Verano) stands on the site of St Lawrence's burial place. It suffered bomb damage in WWII but retains a stunning Cosmati floor and 13th-century frescoed portico.

❷ Explore the Cimitero di Campo Verano

Next door to the Basilica, the **Cimitero di Campo Verano** (📞06 4923 6349; www.cimitericapitolini.it; Piazzale del Verano 1; ⊙7.30am-6pm Apr-Sep, to 5pm Oct-Mar; 🚃Piazzale del Verano) is a strangely moving place. Avenues of grandiose tombs criss-cross the cemetery, Rome's largest, which dates to the Napoleonic occupation of Rome (1804–14).

❸ Chocolate at Said

For a change of scene, search out **Said** (📞06 446 92 04; www.said.it; Via Tiburtina 135; meals €50; ⊙6pm-12.30am Mon, 10am-12.30am Tue-Fri, to 1.30am Sat, to midnight Sun; 🛜; 🚃Via Tiburtina, 🚋Via dei Reti). A delicious hideaway set in a 1920s factory, it's part shop – selling all sorts of exotic chocs – part bar (try the hot chocolate) and part restaurant.

❹ Wine Tasting at Il Sori

Every last salami slice and chunk of cheese has been carefully selected from Italy's finest artisans and small producers at **Il Sori** (📞393 4318661; www.ilsori.it; Via dei Volsci 51; ⊙7.30am-2am

Mon-Sat; 🚃Via Tiburtina), a gourmet wine bar and *bottega* (food shop) that is an unexpected pearl of a stop for dedicated foodies.

❺ Dining at Tram Tram

Achingly hip despite its vintage pedigree, **Tram Tram** (📞06 49 04 16; www.tramtram.it; Via dei Reti 44; meals €35-45; ⊙12.30-3.30pm & 7.30-11.30pm Tue-Sun; 🚃Via Tiburtina, 🚋Via dei Reti) is a wildly popular, old-style trattoria with lace curtains. It's a family-run affair that mixes classical Roman dishes with seafood from Puglia. Book ahead.

❻ Hang Out at Necci

Start your exploration of bar-studded Pigneto at iconic **Necci dal 1924** (📞06 9760 1552; www.necci1924.com; Via Fanfulla da Lodi 68; ⊙8am-2am; 🛜🍴; 🚃Via Prenestina). The old stomping ground of film director Pier Paolo Pasolini, this laid-back spot caters to an eclectic crowd that comes to drink on the leafy terrace or dine on seasonal food.

❼ Speakeasy Cocktails

Cocktails have never been so cool in Rome and chic cocktail bar **Co.So** (📞06 4543 5428; Via Braccio da Montone 80; ⊙7pm-3am Mon-Sat; 🚃Via Prenestina) is the spot in Pigneto to hobnob over 'carbonara sour' cocktails (with pork-fat-infused vodka). Later, duck across the street to **Spirito** (📞327 2983900; www.club-spirito.com; Via Fanfulla da Lodi 53; ⊙7.30pm-3am Wed-Mon; 🚃Via Prenestina), a New York–style speakeasy hidden at the back of sandwich shop.

Explore

Monti & Esquilino

Centred on transport hub Stazione Termini, this is a large and cosmopolitan area that, upon first glance, can seem busy and overwhelming. But hidden among its traffic-noisy streets are some beautiful churches, Rome's best unsung art museum at Palazzo Massimo alle Terme, and any number of trendy bars and restaurants in the fashionable Monti.

The Sights in a Day

☼ Leave the choking chaos of the Termini behind as you enter the hushed halls of the **Museo Nazionale Romano: Palazzo Massimo alle Terme** (p82), one of Rome's best museums. Lose yourself among the sculpture and frescoes before heading over to the **Basilica di Santa Maria Maggiore** (p85) and nearby **Basilica di Santa Prassede** (p87), famous for its glorious Byzantine mosaics. After so much worthy art, treat yourself to lunch at **Panella** (p87).

☼ First stop on the afternoon agenda (but make it after 3pm) is the **Basilica di San Pietro in Vincoli** (p86), which boasts a resident Michelangelo. Afterwards, wander up through Monti, exploring boutiques and ateliers as you make for **Palazzo delle Esposizioni** (p86) to check out an exhibition.

☾ Spend the evening in Monti. Start with dinner at **L'Asino d'Oro** (p88), then take your pick from the area's many bars and cafes – **Ai Tre Scalini** (p87) is always a popular choice.

◉ Top Sight

Museo Nazionale Romano: Palazzo Massimo alle Terme (p82)

♥ Best of Rome

History
Basilica di San Pietro in Vincoli (p86)

Food
Antonello Colonna Open (p87)

Mercato Centrale (p88)

Pasta Chef (p88)

Bars & Nightlife
Ai Tre Scalini (p87)

Architecture
Basilica di Santa Maria Maggiore (p85)

Getting There

Ⓜ **Metro** The Cavour metro stop (line B) is most convenient for Monti, while the Termini (lines A and B), Castro Pretorio (line B) and Vittorio Emanuele (line A) stations are useful for Esquilino.

🚌 **Bus** Termini is the city's main bus hub, connected to places all over the city. Access Monti from buses stopping on Via Nazionale or Via Cavour.

Top Sights
Museo Nazionale Romano: Palazzo Massimo alle Terme

One of Rome's finest museums, this light-filled treasure trove is packed with spectacular classical art. Start your visit on the 2nd floor, so you see its wonders when you're fresh – the sensational frescoes here give a more complete picture of the inside of grand ancient Roman villas than you'll see anywhere else in the world.

👁 Map p84, D2

📞 06 3996 7700

www.coopculture.it

Largo di Villa Peretti 1

adult/reduced €7/3.50

🕙 9am-7.45pm Tue-Sun

Ⓜ Termini

Fresco from Villa Livia depicting a pomegranate tree, Palazzo Massimo alle Terme

Villa Frescoes

On the 2nd floor, magnificent and vibrantly coloured frescoes include scenes from nature, mythology, and domestic and sensual life, using rich, vivid (and expensive) colours. The showstopper is the decoration covering an entire room from Villa Livia, one of the homes of Augustus' wife Livia Drusilla. The frescoes depict a paradisiacal garden full of a wild tangle of roses, violets, pomegranates, irises and camomile under a deep-blue sky. These decorated a summer *triclinium,* a large living and dining area built half underground to provide protection from the heat. The lighting mimics the modulation of daylight and highlights the richness of the millennia-old colours.

Floor Mosaics

The 2nd floor also features some exquisitely fine floor mosaics and rare inlay work from the 13th and 14th centuries. That these mosaics carpeting plush villa floors were trampled on by hundreds upon thousands of aristocratic Romans is utterly scandalous.

Portraits & Bronzes

The ground and 1st floors are devoted to sculpture, examining imperial portraiture as propaganda and including some breathtaking works of art, including the 2nd-century-BC Greek bronzes, the *Boxer* and the *Prince,* a crouching *Aphrodite* from Villa Adriana, the 2nd-century-BC sleeping *Hermaphrodite,* and the idealised vision of the *Discus Thrower.* Also fascinating are the elaborate bronze fittings that belonged to Caligula's ceremonial ships.

☑ Top Tips

▶ Save cents by visiting on the 1st Sunday of the month when museum admission is free.

▶ Rent an audio guide at the main ticket desk for €5.

▶ Tickets, valid for three days, also cover admission to the Terme di Diocleziano, Palazzo Altemps and the Crypta Balbi.

✗ Take a Break

Whatever the time of day, the gourmet food stalls cooking up pretty much everything under the Roman sun – cakes, coffee, lunch, dinner, fast food – at Mercato Centrale (p88) provide perfect post-museum refreshment.

For pizza in a cobbled alley, head to Rome's oldest pizzeria, **Est Est Est** (Da Ricci; ☎ 06 488 11 07; www.anticapizzeria ricciroma.com; Via Genova 32; pizzas €6-15; ⊙7pm-midnight Tue-Sun; ❄; 🚇 Via Nazionale), a 10-minute walk away.

For reviews see

◉	Top Sights	p82
◎	Sights	p85
✕	Eating	p87
🍷	Drinking	p89
⊕	Entertainment	p90
🛍	Shopping	p91

A 0 ——————————— 200 m
0 ——————————— 0.1 miles

Via Volturno

Via Cernaia

🔒 22

Piazza della Repubblica

Museo Nazionale Romano: Terme di Diocleziano

◉ 2

Repubblica Ⓜ

◎ 6

Viale L Einaudi

Repubblica Ⓜ

Via Enrico de Nicola

Piazza de Cinquecer

Ⓟ

Via Modena

Largo di Villa Peretti

Main Bus Station

Via del Viminale

◉

Museo Nazionale Romano: Palazzo Massimo alle Terme

Termini Ⓜ Stazi Term

Via Giovanni Giol

15

Via Firenze

Via Torino

Via Napoli

18

Piazza Beniamino Gigli

Via Massimo d'Azeglio

Via Amendola

Quirinale

Via delle Quattro Fontane

Via Piacenza

Via Genova

Via San Vitale

Via Nazionale

Via Agostino Depretis

Piazza del Viminale

ESQUILINO

✕10

ⓘ

5 ◎ Palazzo delle Esposizioni

Via Palermo

Ministero dell'Interno

Via Cesare Balbo

Piazza dell'Esquilino

Via Farini

Via dell'Esquilino

Via Gioberti

Via Napoleone II

Via del Boschetto

Via Milano

Via Urbana

Basilica di Santa Maria Maggiore

1 ◉

Piazza Santa Maria Maggiore

Via Liberiana

Via Cattan

19

Via di Santa Maria Maggiore

Via dei Capocci

Via Cavour

Via Paolina

Via Carlo Alberto

Via dei Serpenti

12
✕25 🛍20

21 🛍

✕9

Via Panisperna

Via Cimarra

14
🛍

Via dell'Olmata

7 ◎

Basilica di Santa Prassede

Largo Sant' Alfonso

Via d San Vit

✕11

MONTI

Piazza Zingari

Via Urbana

Via Quattro Cantoni

Via Sforza

Via San Martino ai Monti

Largo Brancaccio

13 ✕

Piazza Madonna dei Monti

🛍17

Via degli Zingari

Cavour Ⓜ

Via Giovanni Lanza

Piazza San Martino ai Monti

Via dello Statuto

Via Merulana

8 ◎

🍷
16

🛍24

🛍23

Largo Visconti Venosta

Via Leonina

Via in Selci

Via Cavour

Via degli Annibaldi

Via della Polveriera

4 ◎ Basilica di San Pietro in Vincoli

Via delle Sette Sale

Viale del Monte Oppio

Via Macenate

3 ▼ Domus Aurea

Parco di Traiano

Parco del Colle Oppio

Via Eudossiana

Interior of the Basilica di Santa Maria Maggiore

Sights

Basilica di Santa Maria Maggiore

BASILICA

1 🎯 Map p84, D3

One of Rome's four patriarchal basilicas, this monumental 5th-century church stands on the summit of the Esquiline Hill, on the spot where snow is said to have miraculously fallen in the summer of AD 358. To commemorate the event, every year on 5 August thousands of white petals are released from the basilica's coffered ceiling. Much altered over the centuries, it's an architectural hybrid with 14th-century Romanesque belfry, 18th-century baroque facade, largely baroque interior and a series of glorious 5th-century mosaics. (🗖06 6988 6800; Piazza Santa Maria Maggiore; basilica free, adult/reduced museum €3/2, museum & loggia €5/4; 🕐7am-7pm, loggia guided tours 9.30am-5.45pm; 🚇Piazza Santa Maria Maggiore)

Museo Nazionale Romano: Terme di Diocleziano

MUSEUM

2 🎯 Map p84, D1

The Terme di Diocleziano was ancient Rome's largest bath complex, covering about 13 hectares and able to accommodate some 3000 people. Today its ruins house a branch of the impressive Museo Nazionale Romano. Exhibits, which include memorial inscriptions, bas-reliefs and archaeological arte-facts, provide a fascinating insight into Roman life. Outside, the vast cloister, constructed from drawings by Michelangelo, is lined with classical sarcophagi, headless statues and huge sculptured animal heads, thought to have come from the Foro di Traiano. (☏06 3996 7700; www.coopculture.it; Viale Enrico de Nicola 78; adult/reduced €7/3.50; ⊙9am-7.30pm Tue-Sun; Ⓜ️Termini)

Domus Aurea   ARCHAEOLOGICAL SITE

3 ◉ Map p84, B5

Nero had his Domus Aurea construct-ed after the fire of AD 64 (which he is rumoured to have started to clear the area). Named after the gold that lined its facade and interiors, it was a huge complex covering up to a third of the city. Making full use of virtual reality, superb state-of-the-art guided tours shed light on just how grand the Golden House – a lavish villa with porticoes – was. Advance online res-ervations are obligatory. (Golden House; ☏06 3996 7700; www.coopculture.it; Viale della Domus Aurea; adult/under 6yr €14/free; ⊙9am-4.45pm Sat & Sun; Ⓜ️Colosseo)

Basilica di San Pietro in Vincoli   BASILICA

4 ◉ Map p84, B5

Pilgrims and art lovers flock to this 5th-century basilica for two reasons: to marvel at Michelangelo's colossal *Moses* (1505) sculpture and to see the chains that supposedly bound St Peter when he was imprisoned in the Carcere Mamertino (near the Roman Forum). Access to the church is via a flight of steps through a low arch that leads up from Via Cavour. (Piazza di San Pietro in Vincoli 4a; ⊙8am-12.30pm & 3-7pm summer, to 6pm winter; Ⓜ️Cavour)

Palazzo delle Esposizioni   CULTURAL CENTRE

5 ◉ Map p84, A3

This huge neoclassical palace was built in 1882 as an exhibition centre, though it has since served as head-quarters for the Italian Communist Party, a mess hall for Allied service-men, a polling station and even a public loo. Nowadays it's a splendid cultural hub, with cathedral-scale exhibition spaces hosting blockbuster art exhibitions and sleekly designed art labs, as well as a bookshop, cafe and Michelin-starred restaurant, An-tonello Colonna Open (see opposite), serving a bargain lunch or brunch beneath a dazzling all-glass roof. Oc-casional concerts, performances and film screenings are also held here. (☏06 3996 7500; www.palazzoesposizioni. it; Via Nazionale 194; ⊙10am-8pm Tue-Thu & Sun, to 10.30pm Fri & Sat; 🚌Via Nazionale)

Piazza della Repubblica   PIAZZA

6 ◉ Map p84, C1

Flanked by grand 19th-century neo-classical colonnades, this landmark piazza was laid out as part of Rome's post-unification makeover. It follows the lines of the semicircular *exedra* (benched portico) of Diocletian's baths complex and was originally known as Piazza Esedra. (**M**Repubblica)

Basilica di Santa Prassede

CHURCH

7 Map p84, D4

Famous for its brilliant Byzantine mosaics, this tiny gem of a 9th-century church is dedicated to St Praxedes, an early Christian heroine who hid Christians fleeing persecution and buried those she couldn't save in a well. The position of the well is now marked by a marble disc on the floor of the nave. (06 488 24 56; Via Santa Prassede 9a; 7am-noon & 4-6.30pm; Piazza Santa Maria Maggiore)

Eating

Panella

BAKERY, CAFE €

8 Map p84, D5

Pure heaven for foodies, this enticing bakery is littered with well-used trays of freshly baked pastries loaded with confectioner's custard, wild-cherry fruit tartlets, *pizza al taglio, arancini* and focaccia – the smell alone is heavenly. Grab a bar stool between shelves of gourmet groceries inside or congratulate yourself on scoring a table on the flowery, sun-flooded terrace – one of Rome's loveliest. (06 487 24 35; www.panellaroma.com; Via Merulana 54; meals €7-15; 8am-11pm Mon-Thu, to midnight Fri & Sat, 8.30am-4pm Sun; **M**Vittorio Emanuele)

Ai Tre Scalini

WINE BAR €€

9 Map p84, A4

A firm favourite since 1895, the 'Three Steps' is always packed, with crowds spilling out of the funky violet-painted door and into the street. Tuck into a heart-warming array of cheeses, salami and dishes such as *polpette al sugo* (meatballs with sauce), washed down with superb choices of wine or beer. (06 4890 7495; www.aitrescalini.org; Via Panisperna 251; meals €25; 12.30pm-1am; **M**Cavour)

Antonello Colonna Open

ITALIAN €€€

10 Map p84, A2

Spectacularly set at the back of Palazzo delle Esposizioni, super-chef Antonello Colonna's Michelin-starred restaurant lounges dramatically under a dazzling all-glass roof. Cuisine is new Roman – innovative takes on traditional dishes, cooked wit and flair – and the all-you-can-eat lunch buffet and weekend brunch are unbeatable value. On sunny days, dine alfresco on the rooftop terrace. (06 4782 2641; www.antonellocolonna.it; Via Milano 9a; lunch/brunch €16/30, meals €16-100; 12.30-3.30pm & 8-11pm Tue-Sat, 12.30-3.30pm Sun; Via Nazionale)

Temakinho

SUSHI €€

11 Map p84, A4

In a city where most food is still resolutely (though deliciously) Italian, this Brazilian-Japanese hybrid serving up sushi and ceviche makes for a sensationally refreshing change. As well as delicious, strong caipirinhas, which combine Brazilian *cachaça*, sugar, lime and fresh fruit, there are 'sakehinhas' made with sake. It's very popular; book ahead. (📞 06 4201 6656; www.temakinho.com; Via dei Serpenti 16; meals €40; ⏰ 12.30-3.30pm & 7pm-midnight; Ⓜ Cavour)

L'Asino d'Oro   ITALIAN €€

12 🍴 Map p84, A4

This fabulous restaurant was transplanted from Orvieto, and its Umbrian origins resonate in Lucio Sforza's exceptional cooking. Unfussy yet innovative dishes feature bags of flavourful contrasts, like lamb meatballs with pear and blue cheese. Save room for the equally amazing desserts. Intimate, informal and classy, this is one of Rome's best deals – its lunch menu is a steal. (📞 06 4891 3832; www.facebook.com/asinodoro; Via del Boschetto 73; weekday lunch menu €16, meals €45; ⏰ 12.30-2.30pm & 7.30-11pm Tue-Sat; Ⓜ Cavour)

Pasta Chef   FAST FOOD €

13 🍴 Map p84, A4

'Gourmet street food' is the strapline of this fast-food joint where chefs Mauro and Leopoldo whip up steaming bowls of perfectly cooked pasta laced with carbonara, *pomodoro e basilico* (tomato and basil), bolognese and other classic sauces for a discerning, budget-conscious crowd. There's a veggie lasagne and other

vegetarian options. The dynamic duo also run pasta cooking classes. (📞 06 488 31 98; www.pastachefroma.it; Via Baccina 42; pasta €5-8; ⏰ 12.30-9.30pm Mon-Sat; Ⓜ Cavour)

Aromaticus   HEALTH FOOD €

14 🍴 Map p84, B4

Few addresses exude such a healthy vibe. Set within a shop selling aromatic plants and edible flowers, this inventive little cafe is the perfect place to satisfy green cravings. Its short but sweet menu features lots of creative salads, soups and gaspacho, tartare and carpaccio, juices and detox smoothies – all to stay or go. (📞 06 488 13 55; www.aromaticus.it; Via Urbana 134; meals €10-15; ⏰ 11am-3pm & 6-8.30pm; 📶; Ⓜ Cavour)

Mercato Centrale   FOOD HALL €

15 🍴 Map p84, D2

A gourmet oasis for hungry travellers at Stazione Termini, this dazzling three-storey food hall is the latest project of Florence's savvy Umberto Montano. You'll find breads, pastries, cakes, veggie burgers, fresh pasta, truffles, pizza and a whole lot more beneath towering vaulted 1930s ceilings, as well as some of the city's most prized producers, including Gabriele Bonci (breads, focaccia and pizza), Roberto Liberati (salami), Marcella Bianchi (vegetarian). (www.mercatocentrale.it/roma; Via Giolitti 36, Stazione Termini; snacks/meals from €3/10; ⏰ 7am-midnight; 📶; Ⓜ Termini)

Food stall, Mercato Centrale

Drinking

La Casetta a Monti   CAFE

16 🚇 Map p84, A5

Delicious cakes, pastries and the finest chocolate salami in town is the name of the game at this uber-cute cafe, dolls house is size, run with much love and passion by Eugenio and Alessandro. Find the cafe, all fresh and sassy after a 2017 restyle, in a low-lying house with big windows and foliage-draped facade in the cobbled heart of Monti. There's breakfast, lunch, drinks and music too. (📞06 482 7756; www.facebook.com/lacasettadeimonti; Via

---

☑ Top Tip

Wine Tastings

With beautifully appointed century-old cellars and a chic tasting studio, **Vino Roma** (Map p84, B4; 📞328 487 44 97; www.vinoroma.com; Via in Selci 84g; 2hr tastings per person €50; Ⓜ Cavour) guides novices and experts in tasting wine under the knowledge-able stewardship of sommelier Hande Leimer and her expert team. Also on offer is a wine-and-cheese dinner (€60) with snacks, cheeses and cold cuts to accompany the wines, and bespoke three-hour food tours. Book online.

Local Life
Pasticceria Regoli

At weekends a queue marks the entrance to this elegant chandelier-lit **pasticceria** (Map p84, D4; 📞 06 487 2812; www.pasticceriaregoli.com; Via dello Statuto 60; ⏰ cafe 6.30am-7.45pm Wed-Sun, shop to 8.20pm; M Vittorio Emanuele), much-loved since 1916. Its *crostate* (latticed jam tarts) are iconic, and a *maritozzi con panna* (sweet bread bun filled to bursting with whipped cream) is the down-right wicked speciality to order in the neighbouring cafe – spot the secret hatch hidden in a mirror through which cakes are passed between the two. Excellent ice cream too.

della Madonna dei Monti 62; ⏰ 9.30am-8pm Mon-Thu, to 10pm Fri & Sat, 8.30am-9pm Sun; 🛜; M Cavour)

La Bottega del Caffè   CAFE

18 🟤 Map p84, A4

On one of Rome's prettiest squares in Monti, La Bottega del Caffè – named after a comedy by Carlo Goldoni – is the hot spot in Monti to linger over coffee, drinks, snacks and lunch or dinner. Heaters in winter ensure balmy alfresco action year-round. (📞 06 474 15 78; Piazza Madonna dei Monti 5; ⏰ 8am-2am; 🛜; M Cavour)

Entertainment

Teatro dell'Opera di Roma   OPERA, BALLET

18 ⭐ Map p84, C2

Rome's premier opera house boasts a plush gilt interior, a Fascist 1920s exterior and an impressive history: it premiered Puccini's *Tosca,* and Maria Callas once sang here. Opera and ballet performances are staged between September and June. (📞 06 48 16 01; www.operaroma.it; Piazza Beniamino Gigli 1; ⏰ box office 10am-6pm Mon-Sat, 9am-1.30pm Sun; M Repubblica)

Blackmarket   LIVE MUSIC

19 ⭐ Map p84, B3

A bit outside the main Monti hub, this charming, living-room-style bar filled with eclectic vintage furniture is a small but rambling place, great for sitting back on mismatched armchairs and having a leisurely, convivial drink. It hosts regular acoustic indie and folk gigs, which feel a bit like having a band in your living room. (www.black marketartgallery.it/monti; Via Panisperna 101; ⏰ 7.30pm-2am; M Cavour)

Charity Café   LIVE MUSIC

20 ⭐ Map p84, A4

Think narrow space, spindly tables, dim lighting and laid-back vibe: this is a place to snuggle down and listen to some slinky live jazz and blues.

Civilised, relaxed, untouristy and very Monti. Gigs usually take place from 10pm, with live music and *aperitivo*. (📞06 4782 5881; www.charitycafe.it; Via Panisperna 68; ⏰7pm-2am Tue-Sun; Ⓜ Cavour)

Shopping

Tina Sondergaard
FASHION & ACCESSORIES

21 🔒 Map p84, A4

Sublimely cut and whimsically retro-esque, Tina Sondergaard's handmade threads for women are a hit with fashion cognoscenti, including Italian rock star Carmen Consoli and the city's theatre and TV crowd. You can have adjustments made (included in the price); dresses cost around €150. (📞334 385 07 99; Via del Boschetto 1d; ⏰3-7.30pm Mon, 10.30am-1pm & 1.30-7.30pm Tue-Sat, closed Aug; Ⓜ Cavour)

Feltrinelli International
BOOKS

22 🔒 Map p84, B1

The international branch of Italy's ubiquitous bookseller has a splendid collection of books in English, Italian, Spanish, French, German and Portuguese. You'll find everything from recent bestsellers to dictionaries, travel guides, DVDs and an excellent assortment of maps. (📞06 482 78 78; www.lafeltrinelli.it; Via VE Orlando 84-86; ⏰9am-8pm Mon-Sat, 10.30am-1.30pm & 4-8pm Sun; Ⓜ Repubblica)

Mercato Monti Urban Market
MARKET

23 🔒 Map p84, A4

Vintage clothes, accessories, one-off pieces by local designers: this market in the hip 'hood of Monti is well worth a rummage. (www.mercatomonti. com; Via Leonina 46; ⏰10am-8pm Fri-Sun Sep-Jun; Ⓜ Cavour)

La Bottega del Cioccolato
FOOD

24 🔒 Map p84, A4

Run by the younger generation of a long line of *chocolatiers,* this is an exotic world of scarlet walls and old-fashioned glass cabinets set into black wood, with irresistible smells wafting in from the kitchen and rows of lovingly homemade chocolates on display. Hot chocolate and cups of milk chocolate, hazelnut or eggnog mousse to take away too. (📞06 482 14 73; www.labottegadelcioccolato.it; Via Leonina 82; ⏰9.30am-7.30pm; Ⓜ Cavour)

Abito
FASHION & ACCESSORIES

25 🔒 Map p84, A4

Wilma Silvestre, founder of local label Le Gallinelle, designs elegant clothes with a difference. Here at her Monti boutique you can browse her chic, laid-back styles and buy off the rack. (📞06 488 10 17; www.legallinelle.it; Via Panisperna 61; ⏰11am-8pm Mon-Sat, 3-8pm Sun; Ⓜ Cavour)

Top Sights
Appian Way

Getting There

Ⓜ 🚌 From Stazione Termini: take metro line A to the Colli-Albani metro stop, then bus 660 to the end of the line; or take line B to Circo Massimo then bus 118 to Via Appia Antica.

The Appian Way was known to the Romans as *Regina Viarum* (Queen of Roads). Named after Appius Claudius Caecus, who laid the first 90km section in 312 BC, it was extended in 190 BC to reach Brindisi on the southern Adriatic coast. Today it is one of Rome's most exclusive addresses, a beautiful cobbled thoroughfare flanked by fields, ruins and towering pines.

Villa di Massenzio

The outstanding feature of Maxentius' enormous 4th-century palace complex is the **Circo di Massenzio** (Via Appia Antica 153; 🚌 Via Appia Antica), Rome's best-preserved

Commemorative basreliefs by the side of the Appian Way

ancient racetrack – you can still make out the starting stalls used for chariot races. The 10,000-seat arena was built by Maxentius around 309, but he died before ever seeing a race here. Above the arena are the ruins of his imperial residence.

Mausoleo di Cecilia Metella

Dating to the 1st century BC, this great drum of a **mausoleum** (☑06 3996 7700; www.coopculture.it; Via Appia Antica 161; adult/reduced incl Terme di Caracalla & Villa dei Quintili €6/3; ☺9am-1hr before sunset Tue-Sun; ⊑Via Appia Antica) encloses a burial chamber, now roofless. In the 14th century it was converted into a fort by the Caetani family, who used to frighten passing traffic into paying a toll.

Villa dei Quintili

Towering over green fields, this 2nd-century **villa** (☑06 3996 7700; www.coopculture.it; Via Appia Nuova 1092; adult/reduced incl Terme di Caracalla & Mausoleo di Cecilia Metella €6/3; ☺9am-1hr before sunset Tue-Sun; ⊑Via Appia Antica) is one of Rome's unsung splendors. It was the luxurious abode of two consuls, the Quintili brothers, but its splendour was their downfall: the emperor Commodus had them both killed, taking over the villa for himself. The highlight is the well-preserved baths complex with a pool, *caldarium* (hot bath room) and *frigidarium* (cold bath room).

Catacombe & Basilica di San Sebastiano

A warren of tunnels, the **Catacombe di San Sebastiano** (☑06 785 03 50; www.catacombe.org; Via Appia Antica 136; adult/reduced €8/5; ☺10am-5pm Mon-Sat Jan-Nov; ⊑Via Appia Antica) were the first catacombs to be so called, the name deriving from the Greek *kata* (near) and *kymbas* (cavity), because they were located near a cave. During the persecution of Christians by the emperor Vespasian from AD 258, it's believed that the catacombs were used as a safe haven for the remains of St Peter and St Paul and became a popular pilgrimage site. Above ground, the

☑06 513 53 16

www.parcoappiaantica.it

☺Info Point 9.30am-sunset summer, 9.30am-1pm & 2-5pm Mon-Fri, 9.30am-5pm Sat & Sun winter

⊑Via Appia Antica

☑ Top Tips

▶ The most pleasurable way of exploring the Appian Way is by bicycle. Rent a set of wheels and pick up maps at the Info Point Appia Antica at the northern end of the road.

▶ The Info Point also sells the **Appia Antica Card** (€6), valid seven days and covering admission to three key sights along the way.

✗ Take a Break

Take a coffee or beer break in the tree-shaded garden of **Appia Antica Caffè** (Via Appia Antica 175; ☺9am-sunset); it sells light snacks and prepares picnics too.

Enjoy a garden lunch beneath orange trees at **Il Giardino di Giulia e Fratelli** (Via Appia Antica 176; ☺noon-3pm & 7-11.30pm Tue-Sat).

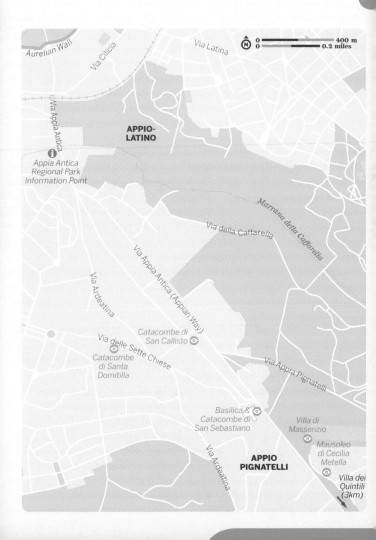

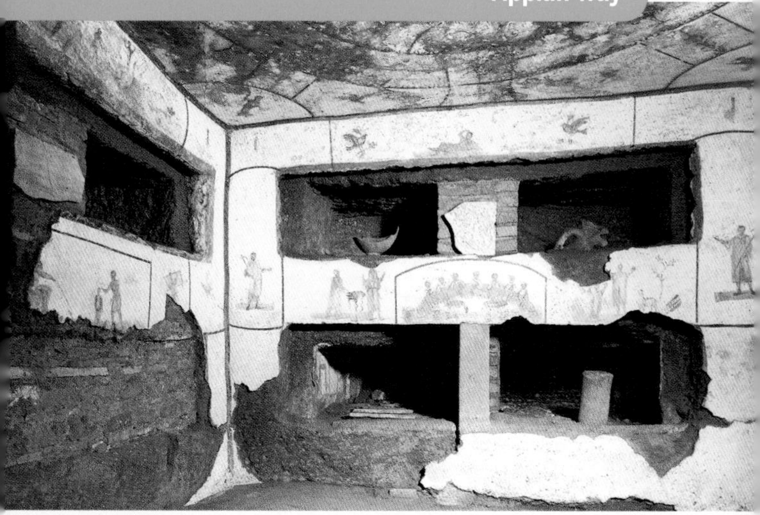

Catacombe di San Callisto

4th-century **basilica** (Via Appia Antica 136; ⌚8am-1pm & 2-5.30pm; 🚌Via Appia Antica) dates mainly from the 17th century. In the Capella delle Reliquie you'll find one of the arrows used to kill St Sebastian and the column to which he was tied. On the other side of the church is a marble slab with Jesus' footprints.

Catacombe di San Callisto

The **Catacombe di San Callisto** (☎06 513 01 51; www.catacombe.roma.it; Via Appia Antica 110-126; adult/reduced €8/5; ⌚9am-noon & 2-5pm Thu-Tue Mar-Jan; 🚌Via Appia Antica) are the largest and busiest of Rome's catacombs. Founded at the end of the 2nd century, they became the official cemetery of the newly established Roman Church. In the 20km of tunnels explored to date, archaeologists have found the tombs of 16 popes, dozens of martyrs and thousands upon thousands of Christians.

Catacombe di Santa Domitilla

Among Rome's largest and oldest, the wonderful **Catacombe di Santa Domitilla** (☎06 511 03 42; www.domitilla.info; Via delle Sette Chiese 282; adult/reduced €8/5; ⌚9am-noon & 2-5pm Wed-Mon mid-Jan–mid-Dec; 🚌Via Appia Antica) stretch for about 17km. They were established on the private burial ground of Flavia Domitilla, niece of the emperor Domitian and a member of the wealthy Flavian family. They contain Christian wall paintings and the haunting underground Chiesa di SS Nereus e Achilleus.

Explore

San Giovanni & Celio

Southeast of the centre, the mighty Basilica di San Giovanni in Laterano is the principal drawcard of the handsome, largely residential San Giovanni district. Nearby, the Celio (Caelian), one of Rome's original seven hills, rises to the south of the Colosseum. A tranquil area of medieval churches and graceful greenery, it's ideal for escaping the crowds but offers little after-hours action.

The Sights in a Day

☀ Start off at the landmark **Basilica di San Giovanni in Laterano** (p98), the focal point of the largely residential San Giovanni neighbourhood. It's easily accessible by metro and quite magnificent, both inside and out. Once you've explored the basilica and surrounding piazza, head down Via di San Giovanni in Laterano towards the Colosseum. Near the bottom, the **Basilica di San Clemente** (p101) is a fascinating church with some thrilling underground ruins. Stop for lunch at cosy **Cafè Cafè** (p103).

☀ Start the afternoon with a walk to the Celio, the green hill that rises south of the Colosseum. There's not a lot to see but the graceful **Villa Celimontana park** (p102; pictured left) is a great place to escape the crowds. While you're in the area, visit the houses of Christian martyrs at **Case Romane** (p102).

☾ Dine at popular **Divin Ostilia** (p103) before heading to a wine bar. Try **Bibenda Wine Concept** (p104) for a great range of vintages or **Il Pentagrappolo** (p104) for a laid-back atmosphere and live music.

⊙ Top Sight
Basilica di San Giovanni in Laterano (p98)

♥ Best of Rome
History
Basilica di San Clemente (p101)

Case Romane (p102)

Basilica di San Giovanni in Laterano (p98)

Food
Aroma (p103)

Bars & Nightlife
Bibenda Wine Concept (p104)

Architecture
Basilica di San Giovanni in Laterano (p98)

Getting There

🚌 **Bus** Useful bus routes include 85 and 87, both of which stop near the Basilica di San Giovanni in Laterano, and 714, which serves San Giovanni.

Ⓜ **Metro** San Giovanni is accessible by metro line A.

🚋 **Tram** Number 3 runs from San Giovanni along Viale Aventino, through Testaccio and on to Trastevere.

Top Sights
Basilica di San Giovanni in Laterano

For a thousand years this monumental cathedral was the most important church in Christendom. Dating to the 4th century, it was the first Christian basilica built in the city and, until the late 14th century, it was the pope's main place of worship. It's still Rome's official cathedral and the pope's seat as the bishop of Rome.

◉ Map p100, E3

Piazza di San Giovanni in Laterano 4

basilica/cloister free/€5 with audio guide

🕑 7am-6.30pm, cloister 9am-6pm

Ⓜ San Giovanni

Interior of the basilica

The Cloister

To the left of the altar, the basilica's 13th-century cloister is a lovely, peaceful place with graceful twisted columns set around a central garden. Lining the ambulatories are marble fragments from the original church, including the remains of a 5th-century papal throne and inscriptions of two papal bulls.

The Facade

Surmounted by 15 7m-high statues – Christ with St John the Baptist, John the Evangelist and the 12 Apostles – Galilei's huge facade is an imposing work of late-baroque classicism. Behind the colossal columns there are five sets of doors in the portico. The central bronze doors were moved here from the Curia in the Roman Forum, while, on the far right, the Holy Door is only opened in Jubilee years.

The Interior

The cavernous interior owes much of its present look to Francesco Borromini, who styled it for the 1650 Jubilee. It's a breathtaking sight with a golden gilt ceiling, a 15th-century mosaic floor, and a wide nave lined with 18th-century sculptures of the apostles.

At the end of the nave, an elaborate Gothic baldachin stands over the papal altar. Dating to the 14th century, this is said to contain the relics of the heads of Sts Peter and Paul. In front, a double staircase leads down to the confessio and the tomb of Pope Martin V (r 1417–31).

At the other end of the basilica, on the first pillar in the right-hand aisle, is an incomplete Giotto fresco. Cock your ear towards the next column, where a monument to Pope Sylvester II (r 999–1003) is said to creak when the death of a pope is imminent.

☑ Top Tips

▶ Make sure you look down as well as up – the inlaid mosaic floor is a wonderful work of art in its own right.

▶ In the cloister, look out for a slab of porphyry on which it's said Roman soldiers threw lots to win the robe of the crucified Christ.

▶ Check out the Giotto fresco on the first column in the right-hand aisle.

▶ There's an information office to the right of the portico, open 9am to 5pm.

✕ Take a Break

There are few recommended eateries right by the basilica so you're better off finishing your tour and heading downhill towards the Colosseum. Here you can lunch on classic trattoria food at Il Bocconcino (p104) or tasty cafe fare at Cafè Cafè (p103).

E

Viale Manzoni

Via Nino Bixio

Via di Quintino

Via Statilia

Via Emanuele Filiberto

Via Galilei

SAN GIOVANNI

Via Tasso

Santuario della
Scala Santa &
Sancta Sanctorum

3

Piazza di Porta
San Giovanni

San Giovanni

Piazzale
Appio

Via Magna Grecia

Via Veio

Via Amiterno

Via Sannio

Via Boiardo

D

Via Ariosto

Via Merulana

Viale Manzoni

Via P Villari

Obelisk

Piazza di
San Giovanni
in Laterano

**Basilica di
San Giovanni
in Laterano**

2

Via
Alfieri

Via
Guicciardini

Via Carlo
Botta

Via A
Poliziano

C

Via Ruggero Bonghi

Piazza
Iside

Via Labicana

Via Crescimbeni

**Basilica di
San Clemente**

10

Via di San Clemente

Via Muratori

Piazza di
San Clemente

Via dei Santi Quattro

14

Via di Santo Stefano Rotondo

Via dell'Amba Aradam

For reviews see

	Top Sights	p98
	Sights	p101
	Eating	p103
	Drinking	p104
	Shopping	p105

Via di Ferretella in Laterano

Via Ipponio

6

**Basilica dei
SS Quattro
Coronati**

**Chiesa di
Santo Stefano
Rotondo**

2

CELIO

Via di Sant'Erasmo

Piazzale
Metronio

Piazza
Porta
Metronia

Via
Mattonia

B

Parco del Colle Oppio

Via della Domus Aurea

7

8

Via di San Clemente

Via Capo
d'Africa

12

Via M
Aurelio

Via Annia

11

Via Ostilia

10

Via Celimontana

13

Via N Salvi

Piazza del
Colosseo

Via Claudia

Via della Navicella

4 Villa
Celimontana

Parco di Porta Capena

Via di Valle delle Camene

**Viale delle Te
di Carac**

A

M Colosseo

Via Celio
Vibenna

Viale del Parco
del Celio

5 Piazza dei Santi
Giovanni Paolo

Case
Romane

Via della Croce

Clivo di
Scauro

400 m

1

2

3

4

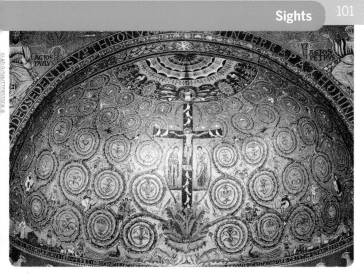

Mosaic, Basilica di San Clemente

Sights

Basilica di San Clemente

BASILICA

1 Map p100, B2

Nowhere better illustrates the various stages of Rome's turbulent past than this fascinating multi-layered church. The ground-level 12th-century basilica sits atop a 4th-century church, which, in turn, stands over a 2nd-century temple to Mithras (p104) and a 1st-century Roman house. Beneath everything are foundations dating from the Roman Republic. (www.basilicasanclemente.com; Piazza San Clemente; excavations adult/reduced €10/5; ⏰9am-12.30pm & 3-6pm Mon-Sat, 12.15-6pm Sun; 🚌Via Labicana)

Chiesa di Santo Stefano Rotondo

CHURCH

2 Map p100, B3

Set in its own secluded grounds, this haunting church boasts a porticoed facade and a round, columned interior. But what really gets the heart racing is the graphic wall decor – a cycle of 16th-century frescoes depicting the tortures suffered by early Christian martyrs. Describing them in 1846, Charles Dickens wrote: 'Such a panorama of horror and butchery no man could imagine in his sleep, though he were to eat a whole pig, raw, for supper'. (www.santo-stefano-rotondo.it; Via di Santo Stefano Rotondo 7; ⏰10am-1pm & 2.30-5.30pm winter, 10am-1pm & 3.30-6.30pm summer; 🚌Via Claudia)

Santuario della Scala Santa & Sancta Sanctorum

CHRISTIAN SITE

3 ◉ Map p100, E2

The Scala Santa, said to be the staircase that Jesus walked up in Pontius Pilate's Jerusalem palace, was brought to Rome by St Helena in the 4th century. Pilgrims consider it sacred and climb it on their knees, saying a prayer on each of the 28 steps. At the top, behind iron grating, is the richly decorated Sancta Sanctorum (Holy of Holies), formerly the pope's private chapel. (www.scala-santa.it; Piazza di San Giovanni in Laterano 14; Scala free, Sancta with/without audio guide €5/3.50; ☺Scala 6am-2pm & 3-7pm summer, to 6pm winter, Sancta Sanctorum 9.30am-12.45pm & 3-4.45pm Mon-Sat; Ⓜ San Giovanni)

Villa Celimontana

PARK

4 ◉ Map p100, B4

With its grassy banks and colourful flower beds, this leafy park is a wonderful place to escape the crowds and enjoy a summer picnic. At its centre is a 16th-century villa housing the Italian Geographical Society, while to the south stands a 12m-plus Egyptian obelisk. (☺7am-sunset; 🚇Via della Navicella)

Case Romane

CHRISTIAN SITE

5 ◉ Map p100, A3

According to tradition, two martyred Roman soldiers, John and Paul, lived in these subterranean houses beneath the **Basilica dei SS Giovanni e Paolo al Celio** (Piazza dei Santi Giovanni e Paolo; ☺8.30am-noon & 3.30-6pm; 🚇Via Claudia) before they were beheaded by the emperor Julian. There's actually no direct evidence for this, although research has revealed that the houses were used for Christian worship. There are more than 20 rooms, many of them richly decorated. Entry is to the side of the basilica on the Clivo di Scauro. (🕿06 7045 4544; www.caseromane.it; Clivo di Scauro; adult/reduced €8/6; ☺10am-1pm & 3-6pm Thu-Mon; 🚇Via Claudia)

Basilica dei SS Quattro Coronati

BASILICA

6 ◉ Map p100, C2

This brooding fortified church harbours some lovely 13th-century frescoes and a delightful hidden cloister, accessible from the left-hand aisle. The frescoes, in the Oratorio di San Silvestro, depict the story of Constantine and pope Sylvester I and the so-called Donation of Constantine (p103), a notorious forged document with which the emperor supposedly ceded control of Rome and the Western Roman Empire to the papacy. To access the Oratorio, ring the bell in the entrance courtyard. (🕿06 7047 5427; Via dei Santi Quattro 20; cloisters €2, Oratorio di San Silvestro €1; ☺basilica 6.30am-12.45pm & 3.30-8pm, cloister 9.45-11.45am & 3.45-5.45pm Mon-Sat; 🚇Via di San Giovanni in Laterano)

Understand
The Donation of Constantine

The most famous forgery in medieval history, the Donation of Constantine is a document with which the emperor Constantine purportedly grants Pope Sylvester I (r 314–35) and his successors control of Rome and the Western Roman Empire, as well as primacy over the holy sees of Antioch, Alexandria, Constantinople, Jerusalem and all the world's churches.

No one is exactly sure when the document was written but the consensus is that it dates to the mid- or late 8th century. Certainly this fits with the widespread theory that the author was a Roman cleric, possibly working with the knowledge of Pope Stephen II (r 752–57).

For centuries the donation was accepted as genuine and used by popes to justify their territorial claims. But in 1440 the Italian philosopher Lorenzo Valla proved that it was a forgery. By analysing the Latin used in the document he was able to show that it was inconsistent with the Latin used in the 4th century.

Eating

Aroma   RISTORANTE €€€

7 Map p100, B1

One for a special occasion, the rooftop restaurant of the Palazzo Manfredi hotel offers once-in-a-lifetime views of the Colosseum and Michelin-starred food that rises to the occasion. Overseeing the kitchen is chef Giuseppe Di Iorio, whose seasonal menus reflect his passion for luxurious, forward-thinking Mediterranean cuisine. (06 9761 5109; www.aromarestaurant.it; Via Labicana 125; meals €120-150; 12.30-3pm & 7.30-11.30pm; Via Labicana)

Divin Ostilia   WINE BAR, TRATTORIA €€

8 Map p100, B1

Ever popular Divin Ostilia is a model wine bar with wooden shelves lined with bottles and a high brick ceiling. It's a well-known spot and its cosy interior gets busy at mealtimes as diners squeeze in to feast on cheese and cured meats, grilled steaks and classic pasta dishes. (06 7049 6526; Via Ostilia 4; meals €30-35; noon-1am; Via Labicana)

Cafè Cafè   BISTRO €

9 Map p100, B2

Cosy, relaxed and welcoming, this cafe-bistro is a far cry from the usual impersonal eateries in the Colosseum area. With its rustic wooden tables, butternut walls and wine bottles, it's a charming spot in which to charge your batteries over an egg and bacon breakfast, a light lunch, or afternoon tea and homemade cake. (☏06 700 87 43; www.cafecafebistrot.it; Via dei Santi Quattro 44; meals €15-20; ☺9.30am-8.50pm; ☐Via di San Giovanni in Laterano)

Il Bocconcino   LAZIO CUISINE €€

10 ⊗ Map p100, B2

One of the better options in the touristy pocket near the Colosseum, this easy-going trattoria stands out for its authentic regional cooking and use of locally sourced seasonal ingredients. Daily specials are chalked up on blackboards or there's a regular menu of classic Roman pastas, grilled meats, fish and imaginative desserts. (☏06 7707 9175; www.ilbocconcino.com; Via Ostilia 23; meals €30-35; ☺12.30-3.30pm & 7.30-11.30pm Thu-Tue; ☐Via Labicana)

Drinking

Bibenda Wine Concept   WINE BAR

11 🍷 Map p100, B2

Wine buffs looking to excite their palate should search out this smart modern *enoteca*. Boasting a white, light-filled interior, it has an extensive list of Italian regional labels and European vintages, as well as a small daily food menu. Wines are available to drink by the glass or buy by the bottle. (☏06 7720 6673; www.wineconcept. it; Via Capo d'Africa 21; ☺noon-3pm & 6pm-midnight Mon-Thu, to 2am Fri & Sat, closed Sat lunch & Sun; ☐Via Labicana)

Il Pentagrappolo   WINE BAR

12 🍷 Map p100, B2

This vaulted, softly lit wine bar is the perfect antidote to sightseeing overload. Join the mellow crowd for an evening of wine, piano music and jazz courtesy of the frequent live gigs. There's also a full menu served at lunch and dinner. (☏06 709 63 01; Via Celimontana 21b; ☺noon-3pm & 6pm-1am Mon-Thu, 6pm-2am Fri-Sun; Ⓜ Colosseo)

Alfresco bar

Coming Out
BAR

13  Map p100, B1

On warm evenings, with lively crowds on the street and the Colosseum as a backdrop, there are few finer places to sip a drink at than this friendly gay bar. It's open all day, but is at its best in the evening when the atmosphere hots up, the cocktails kick in and the drag shows and karaoke nights get under way. (☑06 700 98 71; www. comingout.it; Via di San Giovanni in Laterano 8; ☉7.30am-2am; ☐Via Labicana)

Shopping

Soul Food
MUSIC

14  Map p100, C2

Run by Hate Records, Soul Food is a laid-back record store with an eclectic collection of vinyl that runs the musical gamut, from '60s garage and rockabilly to punk, indie, new wave, folk, funk and soul. You'll also find retro T-shirts, fanzines and other groupie clobber. (☑06 7045 2025; www. haterecords.com; Via di San Giovanni in Laterano 192; ☉10.30am-1.30pm & 3.30-7.30pm Tue-Sat; ☐Via di San Giovanni in Laterano)

Local Life
Ostiense & San Paolo

Packed with post-industrial grit, Ostiense is all about exuberant street art, cutting-edge clubs and cool bars. The presence of a university campus lends it a buzz and its disused factories provide space for all sorts of after-hours hedonism. Traditional sights are thin on the ground but you'll find a fabulous museum housed in a former power plant and the world's third-largest church.

Getting There

Ostiense extends south of the city centre along Via Ostiense.

M Line B runs to Piramide, Garbatella and Basilica San Paolo.

🚌 Routes 23 and 716 serve Via Ostiense.

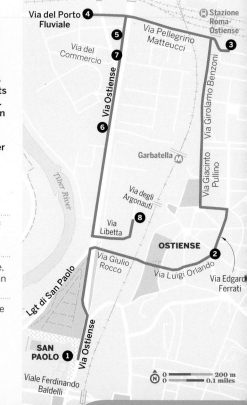

❶ Basilica di San Paolo Fuori le Mura

Start your tour at the **Basilica di San Paolo Fuori le Mura** (✆ 06 6988 0803; www.basilicasanpaolo.org; Via Ostiense 190; adult/reduced €4/3; ⏱ 7am-6.30pm; M Basilica San Paolo), the world's third largest church. Much of the original basilica was destroyed by fire in 1823 but a few features have survived, including the 5th-century triumphal arch, with its heavily restored mosaics, and the Gothic tabernacle.

❷ Garbatella

To experience one of Rome's most idiosyncratic neighbourhoods, make for Garbatella, a colourful garden suburb that was developed in the 1920s and '30s to house people who'd been displaced by fascist construction projects in the city centre.

❸ Lunch at Eataly

For lunch, push on to **Eataly** (www.eataly.net; Piazzale XII Ottobre 1492; meals €10-50; ⏱ shops 9am-midnight, restaurants typically noon-3.30pm & 7-11pm; 🛜; M Piramide), a vast foodie complex with 19 restaurants and cafes.

❹ Street Art on Via del Porto Fluviale

Stroll down Via del Porto Fluviale, home to some of Rome's most inventive street art. Ostiense's abandoned factories boast some impressive murals by the Bolognese artist Blu.

❺ Coffee & Cakes at Andreotti

Treat yourself to afternoon coffee and cake at **Andreotti** (✆ 06 575 07 73; www.andreottiroma.it; Via Ostiense 54; pastries from €1.20; ⏱ 7.30am-10pm; 🚇 Via Ostiense, M Piramide). Local film director Ferzan Ozpetek is a fan and has been known to cast its treats in his films.

❻ Sculpture at Central Montemartini

The **Museo Capitoline Centrale Montemartini** (Museums at Centrale Montemartini; ✆ 06 06 08; www.centralemontemartini.org; Via Ostiense 106; adult/reduced €7.50/6.50, incl Capitoline Museums €16/14, ticket valid 7 days; ⏱ 9am-7pm Tue-Sun; 🚇 Via Ostiense) is a striking outpost of the Capitoline Museums. In an ex-powerplant, ancient sculpture is juxtaposed against engines and furnaces.

❼ Aperitivo at Doppiozeroo

Between 6pm and 9pm, fashion-conscious Romans flock to urbane **Doppiozeroo** (✆ 06 5730 1961; www.doppiozeroo.com; Via Ostiense 68; meals €15; ⏱ 7am-2am; 🚇 Via Ostiense, M Piramide) for its famously lavish *aperitivo* buffet.

❽ Cool Clubbing

Ostiense is serious clubbing country, where top-notch DJs dish out anything from nu-house to thumping techno. Trendy clubs clustered on and around Via Libetta include **Vinile** (www.vinileroma.it), **Circolo Illuminati** (www.circolodegliilluminati.it), **Goa** (www.goaclub.com) and **Neo Club** (www.piovra.it).

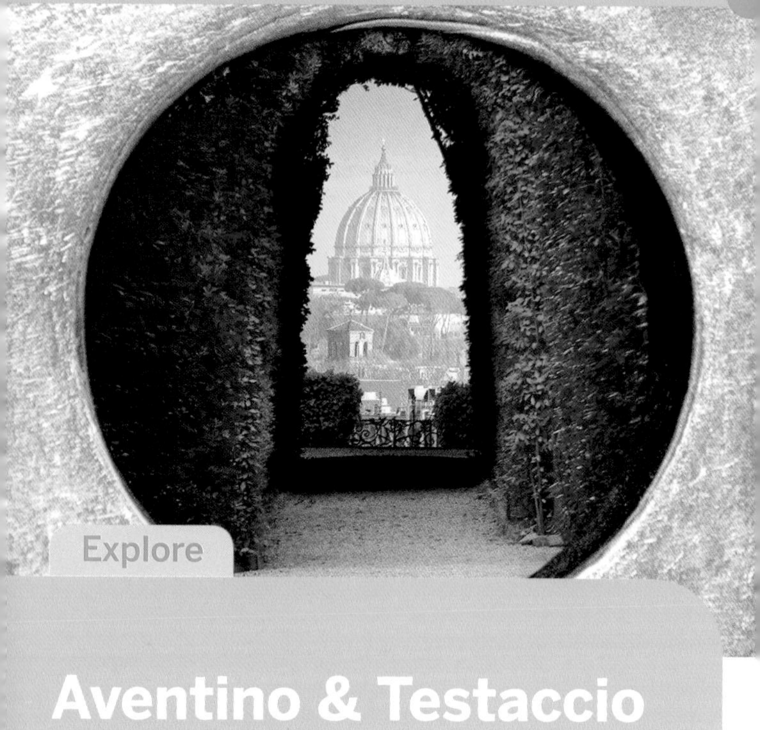

Explore

Aventino & Testaccio

Rising above the mighty ruins of the Terme di Caracalla, the Aventino (Aventine Hill) is a graceful district of villas, lush gardens and austere churches. At the top, Via di Santa Sabina boasts one of Rome's great curiosities – a keyhole view of St Peter's dome (pictured above). Below, the traditional working-class district of Testaccio is a popular nightlife hang-out and a bastion of classical Roman cuisine.

The Sights in a Day

:sun: Start your day exploring the **Terme di Caracalla** (p111), one of ancient Rome's largest bath complexes. Once you're done, push on to Testaccio for a taste of neighbourhood life. Join the locals for a nose around the **Nuovo Mercato di Testaccio** (p113) then grab a takeaway lunch from **Trapizzino** (p113).

:sun: See in the afternoon at the **Cimitero Acattolico per gli Stranieri** (p112), the final resting place of poets Keats and Shelley, before hiking up to the Aventino. It's quite a walk but worth it for the remarkable keyhole view from the **Villa del Priorato di Malta** (p111) and the heart-melting panoramas from **Parco Savello** (p112). While up here, be sure to look into the austere **Basilica di Santa Sabina** (p112).

:crescent_moon: Spend the evening in Testaccio. Dine on fab Roman fare at **Flavio al Velavevodetto** (p113) and then let your hair down at live-music venue **ConteStaccio** (p115).

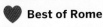 **Best of Rome**

History
Terme di Caracalla (p111)

Food
Da Felice (p113)

Flavio al Velavevodetto (p113)

Mordi e Vai (p113)

Trapizzino (p113)

Architecture
Terme di Caracalla (p111)

Basilica di Santa Sabina (p112)

Shopping
Volpetti (p115)

Nuovo Mercato di Testaccio (p113)

Culture
ConteStaccio (p115)

Getting There

:bus: **Bus** Route 714 serves the Terme di Caracalla.

:M: **Metro** For Testaccio take line B to Piramide. The Aventino is walkable from Testaccio, and Circo Massimo station (line B).

:tram: **Tram** Number 3 runs from San Giovanni along Viale Aventino, through Testaccio and on to Trastevere.

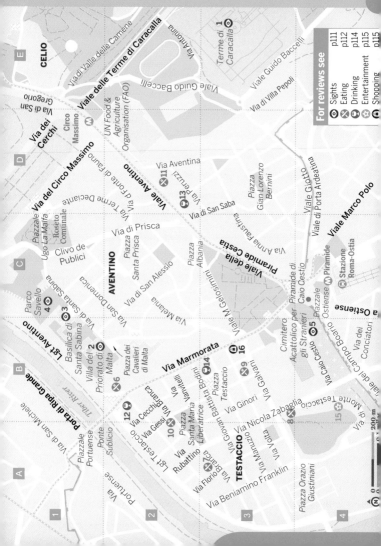

CELIO

Via di Valle delle Camène

Viale delle Terme di Caracalla

Viale Guido Baccelli

Viale Guido Baccelli

Via Antonina

Terme di Caracalla ⊙ 1

Via di Villa Pepoli

Via di San Gregorio

Via dei Cerchi

Circo Massimo Ⓜ

UN Food & Agriculture Organisation (FAO)

Via del Circo Massimo

Via di Fonte di Fauno

Viale Aventino

Via Terme Deciane

Via Aventina

Via di San Saba

Via Peruzzi

⊙ 11

⊙ 13

Piazza Gian Lorenzo Bernini

Viale Giotto

Via di Porta Ardeatina

Viale Marco Polo

Piazzale Ugo La Malfa

Roseto Comunale

Clivo de Publici

Via di Prisca

Piazza Santa Prisca

AVENTINO

Via di San Alessio

Via Melania

Via M Gelsomini

Piazza Albania

Viale della Piramide Cestia

Via Anna Faustina

Piazza Ostiense Ⓜ Piramide

Piramide di Caio Cestio

Stazione Roma-Ostia Ⓜ

Via Ostiense

Parco Savello

⊙ 4

⊙ 3

Basilica di Santa Sabina

Via di Santa Sabina

Via di San Domenica

Lgt Aventino

Villa del Priorato di Malta

⊙ 2

Piazza dei Cavalieri di Malta

✕ 6

Via Marmorata

⊙ 16

✕ 14

✕ 9

Porta di Ripa Grande

Tiber River

Via di San Michele

Piazzale Portuense

Ponte Sublicio

Via Portuense

Lgt Testaccio

🍷 12

Via Cecchina

Via Gessi

Via Vanvitelli

🍷 10

Piazza Santa Maria Liberatrice

Piazza Testaccio

Via Ginori

Via Gavani

Cimitero Acattolico per gli Stranieri

⊙ 5

Via Caio Cestio

Viale del Campo Boario

Via dei Conciator

Via del Monte Testaccio

✪ 8

✪ 15

TESTACCIO

Via Bianca

Via Florio

Via Rubattino

Via Giovan Battista Bodini

Via Manuzio

Via Nicola Zabaglia

Via Volta

Via Beniamino Franklin

Piazza Orazio Giustiniani

200 m

0.1 miles

N

Ruins of Terme di Caracalla

Sights

Terme di Caracalla

ARCHAEOLOGICAL SITE

1 ◉ Map p110, E3

The remains of the emperor Caracalla's vast bath-house complex are among Rome's most awe-inspiring ruins. Inaugurated in AD 216, the original 10-hectare site, which comprised baths, gyms, libraries, shops and gardens, was used by up to 8000 people daily.Most of the ruins are what's left of the central bath house. This was a huge rectangular edifice bookended by two palestre (gyms) and centred on a frigidarium (cold room), where bathers would stop after spells in the warmer tepidarium and dome-capped caldaria (hot room). (✆06 3996 7700; www.coopculture.it; Viale delle Terme di Caracalla 52; adult/reduced €6/3; ◷9am-1hr before sunset Tue-Sun, 9am-2pm Mon; ▣Viale delle Terme di Caracalla)

Villa del Priorato di Malta

HISTORIC BUILDING

2 ◉ Map p110, B1

Fronting an ornate cypress-shaded piazza, the Roman headquarters of the Sovereign Order of Malta, aka the *Cavalieri di Malta* (Knights of Malta), boasts one of Rome's most celebrated views. It's not immediately apparent, but look through the keyhole in the Villa's green door and you'll see the dome of St Peter's Basilica perfectly aligned at the end of a hedge-lined avenue. (Villa Magistrale; Piazza dei Cavalieri di Malta; 🚇Lungotevere Aventino)

Basilica di Santa Sabina   BASILICA

3 🎯 Map p110, C1

This solemn basilica, one of Rome's most beautiful early Christian church-es, was founded by Peter of Illyria in around AD 422. It was enlarged in the 9th century and again in 1216, just be-fore it was given to the newly founded Dominican order – note the tombstone of Muñoz de Zamora, one of the order's founding fathers, in the nave floor. A 20th-century restoration returned it to its original look. (📞06 57 94 01; Piazza Pietro d'Illiria 1; ⏰8.15am-12.30pm & 3.30-6pm; 🚇Lungotevere Aventino)

Parco Savello   PARK

4 🎯 Map p110, C1

Known to Romans as the *Giardino degli Aranci* (Orange Garden), this walled park is a romantic haven. Head down the central avenue, passing towering umbrella pines and lawns of bloom-ing orange trees, to bask in heavenly sunset views of St Peter's dome and the city's rooftops. (Via di Santa Sabina; ⏰7am-6pm Oct-Feb, to 8pm Mar & Sep, to 9pm Apr-Aug; 🚇Lungotevere Aventino)

Cimitero Acattolico per gli Stranieri   CEMETERY

5 🎯 Map p110, B4

Despite the roads that surround it, Rome's 'non-Catholic' Cemetery is a verdant oasis of peace. An air of

Grand Tour romance hangs over the site where up to 4000 people lie buried, including poets Keats and Shelley, and Italian political thinker Antonio Gramsci. Among the grave-stones and cypress trees, look out for the *Angelo del Dolore* (Angel of Grief), a much-replicated 1894 sculpture that US artist William Wetmore Story created for his wife's grave. (www.cemeteryrome.it; Via Caio Cestio 5; voluntary donation €3; ⏰9am-5pm Mon-Sat, to 1pm Sun; 🚇Piramide)

Eating

Romeo e Giulietta   RISTORANTE, PIZZA €€

6 🍴 Map p110, B2

Occupying a former car showroom, this contemporary multi-space food hub is the latest offering from top Roman chef, Cristina Bowerman. The centre of operations is **Romeo Chef & Baker** (📞06 3211 0120 https://romeo.roma.it; meals €40; ⏰10am-2am), a designer deli, cocktail bar and restaurant offering modern Italian and international fare, but there's also **Giulietta Pizzeria** (📞06 4522 9022; https://giuliettapizzeria.it; pizzas €6.50-12; ⏰7pm-midnight daily, noon-3pm Sat-Sun) dishing up sensational wood-fired pizzas, and, a short hop away, **Frigo**, an artisanal gelateria. (Piazza dell'Emporio 28; 🚇Via Marmorata)

Trapizzino   FAST FOOD €

7 Map p110, A3

The original of what is now a grow-ing countrywide chain, this is the birthplace of the *trapizzino,* a kind of hybrid sandwich made by stuffing a cone of doughy focaccia with fillers like *polpette al sugo* (meatballs in tomato sauce) or *pollo alla cacciatore* (stewed chicken). They're messy to eat but quite delicious. (☎06 4341 9624; www.trapizzino.it; Via Branca 88; trapizzini from €3.50; ☺noon-1am Tue-Sun; 🚇Via Marmorata)

Flavio al Velavevodetto   ROMAN €€

8 Map p110, B3

Housed in a rustic Pompeian-red villa set into the side of Monte Testac-cio, a man-made hill of smashed Roman amphorae, this casual eatery is celebrated locally for its earthy, no-nonsense *cucina romana* (Roman cuisine). Expect *antipasti* of cheeses, cured meats and fried titbits, huge helpings of homemade pastas, and uncomplicated meat dishes. (☎06 574 41 94; www.ristorantevelavevodetto.it; Via di Monte Testaccio 97-99; meals €30-35; ☺12.30-3pm & 7.45-11pm; 🚇Via Galvani)

Da Felice   ROMAN €€

9 Map p110, B3

Much loved by local foodies and well-dressed diners, this historic stalwart is famous for its unwavering dedication to Roman culinary tradi-

tions. In contrast to the light-touch modern decor, the menu is pure old school with a classic weekly timetable: *pasta e fagioli* (pasta and beans) on Tuesdays, *bollito di manzo* (boiled beef) on Thursdays, fish on Fridays. Reservations essential. (☎06 574 68 00; www.feliceatestaccio.it; Via Mastro Giorgio 29; meals €30-40; ☺noon-3pm & 7.30-11pm; 🚇Via Marmorata)

Pizzeria Da Remo   PIZZA €

10 Map p110, A2

For an authentic Roman experience, join the noisy crowds here, one of the city's best-known and most popular pizzerias. It's a spartan-looking place, but the fried starters and thin-crust Roman pizzas are the business, and there's a cheerful, boisterous vibe.

○ Local Life
Nuovo Mercato di Testaccio

Testaccio's neighbourhood **market** (Map p110; A3; entrances Via Galvani, Via Beniamino Franklin, Via Volta, Via Manuzio, Via Ghiberti; ☺7am-3.30pm Mon-Sat; 🚇Via Marmorata) hums with morning activity as locals go about their daily shopping for produce, shoes and clothes. Several stalls also serve fantastic street food, including gourmet **Cups** (Box 44; dishes €5-8; ☺8am-4pm Mon-Sat; 🚇Via Galvini) and traditional **Mordi e Vai** (www.mordievai.it; Box 15; panini €3.50-5; ☺8am-3pm Mon-Sat; 🚇Via Galvani).

☑ Top Tip

Opera in the Ruins
The Teatro dell'Opera (www.opera roma.it) stages a summer season of music, opera and ballet among the hulking ruins of the Terme di Caracalla (p111).

Expect to queue after 8.30pm. (📞06 574 62 70; Piazza Santa Maria Liberatrice 44; meals €15; ⏱7pm-1am Mon-Sat; 🚇Via Marmorata)

Il Gelato   GELATO €

11 🍴 Map p110, D2

This is the Aventine outpost of Rome's ice-cream king, Claudio Torcè. His creamy creations are seasonal and preservative free, ranging from the classic to the decidedly not – anyone for green tea or gorgonzola? (Viale Aventino 59; gelato €2-4.50; ⏱10am-midnight summer, 11am-9pm winter; 🚇Viale Aventino)

Drinking

Rec 23   BAR

12 🚇 Map p110, B2

All exposed brick and mismatched furniture, this large, New York–inspired venue caters to all moods, serving *aperitivo*, restaurant meals and a weekend brunch. Arrive thirsty to take on a Bud Spencer, one from the ample list of cocktails, or get to grips with the selection of Scottish whiskies and Latin American rums. Thursday's blues aperitif is a popular weekly appointment. (📞06 8746 2147; www.rec23. com; Piazza dell'Emporio 2; ⏱6.30pm-2am daily & 12.30-3.30pm Sat & Sun; 🚇Via Marmorata)

Casa Manfredi   CAFE

13 🚇 Map p110, D2

Very 'in' when we visited, Casa Manfredi is a good-looking cafe in the wealthy Aventine neighbourhood. Join well-dressed locals for a quick coffee in the gleaming glass and chandelier interior, a light al fresco lunch or chic evening *aperitivo*. It also does a tasty line in artisanal gelato. (📞06 9760 5892; Viale Aventino 93; ⏱7am-9pm; 🚇Viale Aventino, 🚊Viale Aventino)

L'Oasi della Birra   BAR

14 🚇 Map p110, B3

Housed in the Palombi Enoteca, a longstanding bottle shop on Piazza Testaccio, this is exactly what it says it is – an Oasis of Beer. With hundreds of labels, from Teutonic heavyweights to British bitters and Belgian brews, as well as wines, cheeses and cold cuts, it's ideally set up for an evening's quaffing, either in the cramped cellar or piazza-side terrace. (📞06 574 61 22; Piazza Testaccio 41; ⏱4pm-12.30am; 🚇Via Marmorata)

Gelato bar

Entertainment

ConteStaccio
LIVE MUSIC

15 ⭐ Map p110, B4

With an under-the-stars terrace and buzzing vibe, ConteStaccio is one of the top venues on the Testaccio clubbing strip. It's something of a multi-purpose outfit with a cocktail bar, pizzeria and restaurant, but is best known for its free live music. Gigs by emerging groups set the tone, spanning indie, rock, acoustic, funk and electronic genres. (📞06 5728 9712; www.contestaccio.com; Via di Monte Testaccio 65b; ⏰8pm-4am Thu-Sun; 🚌Via Galvani)

Shopping

Volpetti
FOOD & DRINKS

16 🔒 Map p110, B3

This super-stocked deli, considered by many the best in town, is a treasure trove of gourmet delicacies. Helpful staff will guide you through the extensive selection of smelly cheeses, homemade pastas, olive oils, vinegars, cured meats, veggie pies, wines and grappas. It also serves excellent sliced pizza. (www.volpetti.com; Via Marmorata 47; ⏰8.30am-2pm & 4.30-8.15pm Mon-Wed, 8.30am-8.15pm Thu-Sat; 🚌Via Marmorata)

Explore

Trastevere & Gianicolo

With its old-world cobbled lanes, ochre *palazzi* (mansions), ivy-clad facades and boho vibe, ever-trendy Trastevere (pictured above) is one of Rome's most vivacious neighbourhoods. Outrageously photogenic, its labyrinth of backstreets heaves after dark as crowds swarm to its fashionable restaurants, cafes and bars. Rising up behind all this, Gianicolo Hill offers a breath of fresh air and a superb view of Rome.

The Sights in a Day

☀ Start the day by paying homage to St Cecilia, the patron saint of music, at the **Basilica di Santa Cecilia in Trastevere** (p123). Next, head over to Piazza Santa Maria in Trastevere and the neighbourhood's main must-see, the **Basilica di Santa Maria in Trastevere** (p118). For a final flourish before lunch, continue on to **Villa Farnesina** (p124), a palatial Renaissance villa famed for its Raphael frescoes.

☀ After lunch at **Da Enzo** (p121) retrace your footsteps back to **Galleria Corsini** (p123). Next, take an hour or so to chill out in the nearby **Orto Botanico** (p124). Recharged, head up to **Gianicolo Hill** (p124) to admire the superb rooftop views.

☾ Dine on Roman favourites at classic trattoria **Da Teo** (p126) then treat yourself to handmade gelato from **Fior di Luna** (p125). Beer aficionados will want to try the craft beer at **Bir & Fud** (p128).

For a local's evening in Trastevere and Gianicolo, see p120.

⊙ Top Sight

Basilica di Santa Maria in Trastevere (p118)

◯ Local Life

Night Out in Trastevere & Gianicolo (p120)

♥ Best of Rome

Food
Da Augusto (p121)

Da Enzo (p125)

Fior di Luna (p125)

Bars & Nightlife
Freni e Frizioni (p121)

Pimm's Good (p126)

Getting There

🚋 **Tram** From Largo di Torre Argentina, tram 8 runs along the main drag of Viale di Trastevere, ending up at Villa Doria Pamphilj. No 3 also stops at the southern end of Viale Trastevere, connecting with Testaccio (Via Marmorata), Colosseo, San Giovanni and Villa Borghese.

🚌 **Bus** From Termini, bus H runs to Viale di Trastevere, while No 780 runs from Piazza Venezia. For Gianicolo, if you don't fancy the steep steps from Via G Mameli, take bus No 870 from Piazza delle Rovere.

Top Sights
Basilica di Santa Maria in Trastevere

This glittering church is said to be the oldest church in Rome dedicated to the Virgin Mary. Its facade is decorated with a beautiful medieval mosaic depicting Mary feeding Jesus surrounded by 10 women bearing lamps. Two are veiled and hold extinguished lamps, symbolising widowhood, while the lit lamps of the others represent their virginity.

◉ Map p122, B3

☎ 06 581 4802

Piazza Santa Maria in Trastevere

⊙ 7.30am-9pm Sep-Jul, 8am-noon & 4-9pm Aug

🚊 Viale di Trastevere, 🚊 Viale di Trastevere

Facade and balustrade of the basilica

Construction

The church was first constructed in the early 3rd century over the spot where, according to legend, a fountain of oil miraculously sprang from the ground. Its current Romanesque form, including the bell tower and glittering facade, is the result of a 12th-century revamp. The portico was added later by Carlo Fontana in 1702, with its balustrade decorated with statues of four popes.

Mosaics

Inside, it's the golden 12th-century mosaics that stand out. In the apse, look out for the dazzling depiction of Christ and his mother flanked by various saints and, on the far left, Pope Innocent II holding a model of the church. Beneath this is a series of six mosaics by Pietro Cavallini (c 1291) illustrating the life of the Virgin.

Interior Design

Note the 21 Roman columns, some plundered from the Terme di Caracalla; the wooden ceiling designed in 1617 by Domenichino; and, on the right of the altar, a spiralling Cosmati candlestick, on the exact spot where the oil fountain is said to have sprung. The Cappella Avila is also worth a look for its stunning 17th-century dome. The spiralling Cosmatesque floor, a re-creation of the 13th-century original, was relaid in the 1870s.

☑ **Top Tips**

▶ Allow plenty of time to linger on the piazza in front of the church afterwards – it's Trastevere's focal square and a prime people-watching spot.

▶ Visit early in the morning or at the end of the day when the softer light shows off the beautiful Romanesque facade (currently under wraps as painstaking restoration takes place).

✕ **Take a Break**

Grab a cappuccino or a glass of Rome's cheapest beer at Bar San Calisto (p121), a staunchly local haunt just footsteps from the touristy church square.

Tuck into some of the best Roman cuisine in Trastevere at Da Augusto (p121); arrive at 12.30pm on the dot to ensure a table.

Local Life
Night Out in Trastevere & Gianicolo

With its enchanting lanes, vibrant piazzas and carnival atmosphere, Trastevere is one of the city's favourite after-dark hang-outs. Foreigners love it, but it's also a local haunt and Romans come here in swaths, particularly on balmy summer nights when street sellers set up camp on the picturesque alleyways and bar crowds spill out onto the streets.

1 Views on the Gianicolo
The early evening is a good time to enjoy sweeping panoramic views from the Gianicolo. This leafy hill, Rome's highest, was the scene of vicious fighting during Italian unification but is now a tranquil, romantic spot. Lap up the vibe with a drink from **Bar Stuzzichini** (⏰7.30am-1am or 2am; 🚌Passeggiata del Gianicolo) on Piazzale Giuseppe Garibaldi.

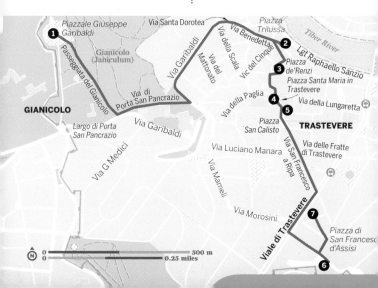

❷ Aperitivo at Freni e Frizioni

Once back down in the fray, head to **Freni e Frizioni** (✆06 4549 7499; www.frenifrizioni.com; Via del Politeama 4-6; ⏲7pm-2am; ◫Piazza Trilussa) for an *aperitivo*. This perennially cool bar pulls in a spritz-loving young crowd that swells onto the small piazza outside to sip cocktails (from €10) and fill up at the bar buffet (7pm to 10pm).

❸ Dinner at Da Augusto

For a real Trastevere dining experience, bag one of the rickety outside tables at **Da Augusto** (✆06 580 37 98; Piazza de' Renzi 15; meals €25; ⏲12.30-3pm & 8-11pm; ◫Viale di Trastevere, ◫Viale di Trastevere) and tuck into some truly fabulous mamma-style cooking on one of Trastevere's prettiest piazza terraces. Hearty portions of all the Roman classics are dished up here as well as lots of rabbit, veal, hare and *pajata* (calf intestines). Winter dining is around vintage formica tables in a bare-bones interior, unchanged for decades. Be prepared to queue. Cash only.

❹ Hanging Out on Piazza di Santa Maria in Trastevere

Trastevere's focal square, **Piazza di Santa Maria in Trastevere** (◫Viale di Trastevere, ◫Viale di Trastevere), is a prime people-watching spot. By day it's full of chatting locals and guidebook-toting tourists but by night the foreign students, young Romans and out-of-towners move in. The octagonal fountain is of Roman origin and was restored by Carlo Fontana in 1692.

❺ Chocolate at Bar San Calisto

Those in the know head to **Bar San Calisto** (Piazza San Calisto 3-5; ⏲6am-2am Mon-Sat; ◫Viale di Trastevere, ◫Viale di Trastevere), a down-at-heel institution popular with everyone from intellectuals to keeping-it-real Romans, alcoholics and American students. It's famous for its chocolate – hot with cream in winter, with gelato in summer – and is known across Rome to serve the cheapest beer in town.

❻ Catch a Film at Nuovo Sacher

Join Rome's passionate cinephiles at the **Nuovo Sacher** (✆06 581 81 16; www.sacherfilm.eu; Largo Ascianghi 1; ◫Viale di Trastevere, ◫Viale di Trastevere), a small cinema owned by cult Roman director Nanni Moretti. A well-known venue for film-related events, it's the perfect place to catch the latest European arthouse offering, with films regularly screened in their original language.

❼ Blues at Big Mama

To wallow in the Eternal City blues, there's only one place to go – **Big Mama** (✆06 581 25 51; www.bigmama.it; Vicolo di San Francesco a Ripa 18; ⏲9pm-1.30am, shows 10.30pm, closed Jun-Sep; ◫Viale di Trastevere, ◫Viale di Trastevere), a cramped Trastevere basement. There are weekly residencies from well-known Italian musicians, and frequent blues, jazz, funk, soul and R&B concerts by international artists.

0 _____ 200 m
0 _____ 0.1 miles

Via Giulia

Via dei Pettinari

Lgt dei Tebaldi

Lgt della Farnesina

Via dei Riari

Via della Lungara

Galleria Corsini **2**

3 Villa Farnesina

5 Orto Via Corsini Botanico

Tiber River

Ponte Sisto

Piazza Trilussa

Via delle Zoccolette

Lgt dei Vallati

Lgt Raphaello Sanzio

Via Arenula

Lgt de Cenci

Ponte Garibaldi

Isola Tiberina

Lgt degli Anguillara

Gianicolo (Janiculum)

Via Garibaldi

Via del Mattonato

12 Via Benedetta

Vic del Bologna

Piazza della Scala

16

7 **14** Via dei Cinque

Via del Politeama

20

22 **10**

Via della Pelliccia

Via Moro

Via Renella

Piazza Sant'Egidio

Piazza Santa Maria in Trastevere

Piazza della Paglia

Via della Lungaretta

Piazza Sonnino

Piazza Belli

Via della Lungaretta

Ponte Cestio

Basilica di Santa Maria in Trastevere

Via della Paglia

Piazza San Calisto

13

Piazza di Piscinula

Gianicolo Hill

6 Piazza San Pietro in Montorio

4 Villa Doria Pamphilj

15 Via Garibaldi

Via G Venzan

Via G Mameli

Via Luciano Manara

TRASTEVERE

Via delle Fratte di Trastevere

Via di Fienaroli

Via di San Gallicano

Via G C Santini

9

Via dei Salumi

8

Via dei Genovesi

11

Via dei Vascell

Piazza San Cosimato

19

Via San Francesco a Ripa

Piazza Mastai

Basilica di Santa Cecilia in Trastevere

1 Piazza Santa Cecilia

Via della Luce

Piazza de' Mercanti

Via Sacchi

Viale Glorioso

Via Dandolo

Via F Casini

Via Dandolo

Via Morosini

Viale di Trastevere

Via Anicia

Via della Madonna dell'Orio

Via di San Michele

Porta di Ripa Grande

17 Piazza di San Francesco d'Assisi

Tiber River

21 Piazzale Portuense

Piazza Porta Portese

Piazza Bernardino da Feltre

Via Portuense

Ponte Sublicio

Lgt Aventino

Piazza dell'Emporio

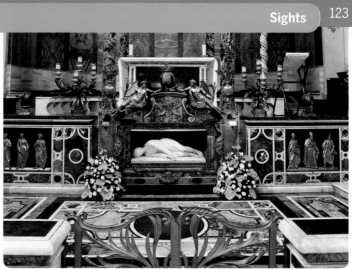

Altar of the Basilica di Santa Cecilia in Trastevere

Sights

Basilica di Santa Cecilia in Trastevere
BASILICA

1 ⦿ Map p122, D4

The last resting place of the patron saint of music features Pietro Cavallini's stunning 13th-century fresco, in the nuns' choir of the hushed convent adjoining the church. Inside the church itself, Stefano Maderno's mysterious sculpture depicts St Cecilia's miraculously preserved body, unearthed in the Catacombs of San Callisto in 1599. You can also visit the excavations of Roman houses, one of which was possibly that of Cecilia. (📞06 589 9289; www.benedettinesanta cecilia.it; Piazza di Santa Cecilia; fresco & crypt each €2.50; ⏱basilica & crypt 10am-1pm & 4-7pm, fresco 10am-12.30pm Mon-Sat; 🚇Viale di Trastevere, 🚋Viale di Trastevere)

Galleria Corsini
GALLERY

2 ⦿ Map p122, A1

Once home to Queen Christina of Sweden, whose richly frescoed bedroom witnessed a steady stream of male and female lovers, the 16th-century Palazzo Corsini was designed by Ferdinando Fuga in grand Versailles style, and houses part of Italy's national art collection. Highlights include Caravaggio's mesmerising *San Giovanni Battista* (St John the Baptist), Guido Reni's unnerving *Salome con la Testa di San Giovanni Battista* (Salome with the Head of John the Baptist), and Fra Angelico's Corsini Triptych, plus works by Rubens, Poussin and Van Dyck. (Palazzo Corsini; 📞06 6880 2323; www.barberinicorsini.org; Via della Lungara 10; adult/reduced €5/2.50, incl Palazzo Barberini €10/5; ⏰8.30am-7.30pm Wed-Mon; 🚌Lungotevere della Farnesina)

Villa Farnesina
HISTORIC BUILDING

3 ◎ Map p122, A1

The interior of this gorgeous 16th-century villa is fantastically frescoed from top to bottom. Several paintings in the Loggia of Cupid and Psyche and the Loggia of Galatea, both on the ground floor, are attributed to Raphael. On the 1st floor, Peruzzi's dazzling frescoes in the Salone delle Prospettive are a superb illusionary perspective of a colonnade and panorama of 16th-century Rome. (📞06 6802 7268; www.villafarnesina.it; Via della Lungara 230; adult/reduced €6/5, guided tour €4; ⏰9am-2pm Mon-Sat, to 5pm 2nd Sun of the month; 🚌Lungotevere della Farnesina)

Villa Doria Pamphilj
MONUMENT, PARK

4 ◎ Map p122, A3

Lorded over by the 17th-century Villa Doria Pamphilj is Rome's largest landscaped park – many a Roman's favourite place to escape the city noise and bustle. Once a vast private estate, it was laid out around 1650 for Prince Camillo Pamphilj, nephew of Pope Innocent X. It's a huge expanse of rolling parkland, shaded by Rome's

distinctive umbrella pines. At its centre is the prince's summer residence, Casino del Belrespiro (used for official government functions today), with its manicured gardens and citrus trees. (⏰sunrise-sunset; 🚌Via di San Pancrazio)

Orto Botanico
GARDENS

5 ◎ Map p122, A2

Formerly the private grounds of Palazzo Corsini, Rome's 12-hectare botanical gardens are a little-known, slightly neglected gem and a great place to unwind in a tree-shaded expanse covering the steep slopes of the Gianicolo. Plants have been cultivated here since the 13th century and the current gardens were established in 1883, when the grounds of Palazzo Corsini were given to the University of Rome. They now contain up to 8000 species, including some of Europe's rarest plants. (Botanical Garden; 📞06 4991 7107; Largo Cristina di Svezia 24; adult/reduced €8/4; ⏰9am-6.30pm Mon-Sat Apr-Oct, to 5.30pm Nov-Mar; 🚌Lungotevere della Farnesina, Piazza Trilussa)

Gianicolo Hill
HILL

6 ◎ Map p122, A3

The verdant hill of Gianicolo is dotted by monuments to Garibaldi and his makeshift army, who fought pope-backing French troops in one of the fiercest battles in the struggle for Italian unification on this spot in 1849. The Italian hero is commemorated with a massive **monument** (🚌Passeggiata del Gianicolo) in

Piazzale Giuseppe Garibaldi, while his Brazilian-born wife, Anita, has her own **equestrian monument** (🚌Passeggiata del Gianicolo) about 200m away in Piazzale Anita Garibaldi; she died from malaria, together with their unborn child, shortly after the siege. (Janiculum)

Eating

La Prosciutteria   TUSCAN €

7 🍽 Map p122, B2

For a gratifying taste of Tuscany in Rome, consider lunch or a decadent *aperitivo* at this Florentine *prosciutteria* (salami shop). Made-to-measure *taglieri* (wooden chopping boards) come loaded with different cold cuts, cheeses, fruit and veg and are best devoured over a glass of Brunello di Montalcino or simple Chianti Classico. Bread comes in peppermint-green tin saucepans and dozens of hams and salami dangle overhead. (📞06 6456 2839; www.laprosciutteria.com/roma-trastevere; Via della Scala 71; chopping board €5 per person; ⏰11am-11.30pm; 🚌Piazza Trilussa)

Da Enzo   TRATTORIA €

8 🍽 Map p122, D3

Vintage buttermilk walls, red-checked tablecloths and a traditional menu featuring all the Roman classics: what makes this staunchly traditional trattoria exceptional is its careful sourcing of local, quality products, many from nearby farms in Lazio. The seasonal,

deep-fried Jewish artichokes and the *pasta cacio e pepe* (cheese-and-black-pepper pasta) in particular are among the best in Rome. (📞06 581 22 60; www.daenzoal29.com; Via dei Vascellari 29; meals €30; ⏰12.30-3pm & 7-11pm Mon-Sat; 🚌Viale di Trastevere, 🚊Viale di Trastevere)

Panattoni   PIZZA €

9 🍽 Map p122, C3

Also called 'ai Marmi' or *l'obitorio* (the morgue) because of its vintage marble-slab tabletops, this is Trastevere's most popular pizzeria. Think super-thin pizzas, a clattering buzz, testy waiters, a street terrace and some fantastic fried starters – the *supplì* (Roman rice ball), *baccalà* (salted cod) and zucchini flowers are all heavenly. (Ai Marmi; 📞06 580 09 19; Viale di Trastevere 53; pizzas €6.50-9; ⏰6.30pm-1am Thu-Tue; 🚌Viale di Trastevere, 🚊Viale di Trastevere)

🔍 Local Life
Fior di Luna

For many Romans busy little **Fior di Luna** (Map p122, C3; 📞06 6456 1314; http://fiordiluna.com; Via della Lungaretta 96; gelato from €1.70; ⏰11.30am-11.30pm Easter-Oct, to 9pm Tue-Sun Nov-Easter; 🚌Viale di Trastevere, 🚊Viale di Trastevere) makes the best handmade gelato and sorbet in the world. Produced in small batches using natural, seasonal ingredients, favourites include walnut and honey, blueberry yoghurt, kiwi (complete with seeds) and pistachio.

Local Life
Grattachecca

It's summertime, the living is easy, and Romans like nothing better in the sultry evening heat than to amble down to the river and partake of some *grattachecca* (crushed ice covered in fruit and syrup). It's the ideal way to cool down and there are kiosks along the riverbank satisfying this very Roman need; try **Sora Mirella Caffè** (Map p122, D3; Lungotevere degli Anguillara; grattachecca €3-6; ⊙11am-3am May-Sep; 🚊Lungotevere degli Anguillara), next to Ponte Cestio.

Forno La Renella
BAKERY €

10 🍴 Map p122, B2

Watch urban pizza masters at work behind glass at this historic Trastevere bakery, a fantastic space to hang out in with its wood-fired ovens, bar-stool seating and heavenly aromas of pizza (€9 to €18 per kilo), bread and biscuits baking throughout the day. Piled-high toppings (and fillings) vary seasonally, to the joy of everyone from punks with big dogs to old ladies with little dogs. It's been in the biz since 1870. (📞06 581 72 65; www.panificiolarenella.com; Via del Moro 15-16; pizza slices from €2.50; ⊙7am-2am Tue-Sat, to 10pm Sun & Mon; 🚊Piazza Trilussa)

Da Teo
TRATTORIA €€

11 🍴 Map p122, D3

One of Rome's classic trattoria, Da Teo buzzes with locals digging into steaming platefuls of Roman standards, such as carbonara, *pasta cacio e pepe* (cheese-and-black-pepper pasta) and the most fabulous seasonal artichokes out – both Jewish (deep-fried) and Roman-style (stuffed with parsley and garlic, and boiled). In keeping with hardcore trattoria tradition, Teo's homemade gnocchi is only served on Thursday. Reservations essential. (📞06 581 83 55; www.trattoriadateo.it; Piazza dei Ponziani 7; meals €30; ⊙12.30-3pm & 7.30-11.30pm Mon-Sat; 🚊Viale di Trastevere, 🚊Viale di Trastevere)

Drinking

Pimm's Good
BAR

12 🚇 Map p122, B2

'Anyone for Pimm's' is the catchline of this eternally popular bar with part red-brick ceiling that does indeed serve Pimm's – the classic way or in a variety of cocktails (€10). The party-loving guys behind the bar are serious mixologists and well-crafted cocktails is their thing. Look for the buzzing street-corner pavement terrace – lit up in winter with flaming outdoor heaters. (📞06 9727 7979; www.facebook.com/pimmsgood; Via di Santa Dorotea 8; ⊙10am-2am; 🛜; 🚊Piazza Trilussa)

Keyhole
COCKTAIL BAR

13 🚇 Map p122, C3

The latest in a growing trend of achingly hip, underground speakeasies in Rome, Keyhole ticks all the boxes: no identifiable name or signage outside

Alfresco dining in Trastevere

the bar; a black door smothered in keys; and Prohibition-era decor including leather Chesterfield sofas, dim lighting and an electric craft cocktail menu. Not sure what to order? Ask the talented mixologists to create your own bespoke cocktail from around €10. (Via Arco di San Calisto 17; ⏰10pm-2am; 🚋Viale di Trastevere, 🚋Viale di Trastevere)

Rivendita Libri, Cioccolata e Vino
COCKTAIL BAR

14 🚇 Map p122, B2

There is no finer – or funnier – spot in the whole of Rome for a swift French Kiss, Orgasm or One Night Stand than this highly inventive

cocktail bar, packed every night from around 10pm with a fun-loving, post-dinner crowd. Cocktails are served in miniature chocolate cups, filled with various types of alcohol and topped with whipped cream. (📞06 5830 1868; www.facebook.com/cioccolateriatrastevere; Vicolo del Cinque 11a; shot €3-5; ⏰7pm-2am Mon-Fri, 2pm-2am Sat & Sun; 🚋Piazza Trilussa)

Il Baretto
BAR

15 🚇 Map p122, A3

Venture a little way up the Gianicolo, up a steep flight of steps from Trastevere – go on, it's worth it. Because there you'll discover this good-looking cocktail bar where the basslines

Understand
Salute!

- -

Aperitivo A Milanese trend from that Romans have taken up with gusto, *aperitivo* is a pre-dinner drink accompanied by a buffet of snacks offered in bars and some restaurants, usually from around 6pm till 9pm. Cost is around €5 to €10 for a drink and unlimited platefuls. Many students and budget-conscious Romans turn *aperitivo* into *apericena* (a replacement for dinner).

Enoteche The *enoteca* (wine bar) was where the old boys from the neighbourhood used to drink rough local wine poured straight from the barrel. Nowadays wine bars tend to be sophisticated but still atmospheric places, offering Italian and international vintages, delicious cheeses and cold cuts.

Bars Rome's bars range from regular Italian cafe-bars that have seemingly remained the same for centuries, to chic, carefully styled places made for esoteric cocktails and laid-back, perennially popular haunts – such as Freni e Frizioni (p121) – that have a longevity rarely seen in other cities.

are meaty, the bar staff hip, and the interior a mix of vintage and pop art. (☎06 589 60 55; www.ilbarettoroma.com; Via Garibaldi 27; ☉7am-2am Mon-Sat; ☒Via Garibaldi)

Bir & Fud

CRAFT BEER

16 Ⓟ Map p122, B2

On a narrow street lined with raucous drinking holes, this brick-vaulted bar-pizzeria wins plaudits for its outstanding collection of craft *bir* (beer), many on tap, and equally tasty *fud* (food) for when late-night munchies strike. Its Neapolitan-style wood-fired pizzas are particularly excellent. (☎06 589 40 16; www.birandfud.it; Via Benedetta 23; ☉noon-2am; ☒Piazza Trilussa)

Entertainment

Lettere Caffè

LIVE MUSIC

17 ⭐ Map p122, C4

Like books? Poetry? Blues and jazz? Then you'll love this place, a clutter of bar stools and books, where there are regular live gigs, poetry slams, comedy and gay nights, plus DJ sets playing electronic, indie and new wave. *Aperitivo,* with a tempting vegetarian buffet, is served between 7pm and 9pm. (☎340 004 41 54; www.letterecaffe.org; Vicolo di San Francesco a Ripa 100-101; ☉6pm-2am, closed mid-Aug–mid-Sep; ☒Viale di Trastevere, ☒Viale di Trastevere)

Shopping

Biscottificio Innocenti FOOD

18 🔒 Map p122, D3

For homemade biscuits, bite-sized meringues and tiny fruit tarts, there is no finer address in Rome than this vintage *biscottificio* with ceramic-tiled interior, fly-net door curtain and a set of old-fashioned scales on the counter to weigh out biscuits (€16 to €24 per kilo). The shop has been run with much love and passion for several decades by the ever-dedicated Stefania. (📞06 580 39 26; www.facebook. com/biscottificioInnocenti; Via delle Luce 21; ⏰8am-8pm Mon-Sat, 9.30am-2pm Sun; 🚊Viale di Trastevere, 🚊Viale di Trastevere)

Antica Caciara Trasteverina FOOD & DRINKS

19 🔒 Map p122, B4

The fresh ricotta is a prized possession at this century-old deli, and it's all usually snapped up by lunchtime. If you're too late, take solace in the to-die-for *ricotta infornata* (oven-baked ricotta), 35kg wheels of famous, black-waxed *pecorino romano* DOP (€16.50 per kilo), and aromatic garlands of *guanciale* (pig's jowl) begging to be chopped up, pan-fried and thrown into the perfect carbonara. (📞06 581 28 15; www.anticacaciara.it; Via San Francesco a Ripa 140; ⏰7am-2pm & 4-8pm Mon-Sat; 🚊Viale di Trastevere, 🚊Viale di Trastevere)

Benheart FASHION & ACCESSORIES

20 🔒 Map p122, B2

From the colourful resin floor papered with children's drawings to the vintage typewriter, dial-up telephone and old-fashioned tools decorating the interior, everything about this artisanal leather boutique is achingly cool. Benheart, a young Florentine designer, is one of Italy's savviest talents and his fashionable handmade shoes (from €190) and jackets for men and women are glorious. (📞06 5832 0801; www.benheart.it; Via del Moro 47; ⏰11am-11pm; 🚊Piazza Triussa)

Porta Portese Market MARKET

21 🔒 Map p122, C5

To see another side of Rome, head to this mammoth flea market. With thousands of stalls selling everything from rare books and fell-off-a-lorry bikes to Peruvian shawls and MP3 players, it's crazily busy and a lot of fun. Keep your valuables safe and wear your haggling hat. (Piazza Porta Portese; ⏰6am-2pm Sun; 🚊Viale di Trastevere, 🚊Viale di Trastevere)

Almost Corner Bookshop BOOKS

22 🔒 Map p122, B2

This is how a bookshop should look: a crammed haven full of rip-roaring reads, with every millimetre of wall space containing English-language fiction and nonfiction (including children's) and travel guides. Heaven to browse. (📞06 583 69 42; Via del Moro 45; ⏰10am-8pm Mon-Sat, 11am-8pm Sun; 🚊Piazza Trilussa)

Explore

Vatican City & Prati

The Vatican, the world's smallest sovereign state, sits over the river from the historic centre. Centred on St Peter's Basilica, it boasts some of Italy's most revered artworks, many housed in the vast Vatican Museums (home of the Sistine Chapel), as well as batteries of over-priced restaurants and souvenir shops. Nearby, the landmark Castel Sant'Angelo looms over the Borgo district and upscale Prati offers excellent accommodation, eating and shopping.

The Sights in a Day

Beat the queues and get to the **Vatican Museums** (p132) at the crack of dawn. These museums house one of the world's great art collections, and while you'll never manage to see everything in one visit, you'll want to check out the **Cortile Ottagono** (p133), home to some amazing classical sculpture, the vibrantly frescoed **Stanze di Rafaello** (p135) and, of course, the **Sistine Chapel** (p135). Afterwards, reflect on what you've seen over a light lunch at **Il Sorpasso** (p144).

After lunch, head to **St Peter's Square** (p142; pictured left), the dramatic gateway to **St Peter's Basilica** (p136), the Vatican's imperious showcase church. Explore the awe-inspiring marble-clad interior and climb the dome before heading down Via della Conciliazione to round off the afternoon at the landmark **Castel Sant'Angelo** (p142).

Come evening, treat yourself to some modern Roman cuisine at **Ristorante L'Arcangelo** (p144), before retiring to jazz mecca **Alexanderplatz** (p145) to see out the day with a concert.

👁 Top Sights

Vatican Museums (p132)

St Peter's Basilica (p136)

💜 Best of Rome

History
St Peter's Basilica (p136)

Food
Fa-Bìo (p143)

Fatamorgana (p144)

Architecture
St Peter's Basilica (p136)

St Peter's Square (p142)

Culture
Alexanderplatz (p145)

Getting There

🚌 **Bus** From Termini, bus 40 is the quickest to the Vatican. You can also take the 64, which runs a similar route but stops more often. Bus 81 runs to Piazza del Risorgimento, passing through San Giovanni and the *centro storico* (historic centre).

Ⓜ **Metro** Take metro line A to Ottaviano-San Pietro. From the station, signs direct you to St Peter's.

🚊 **Tram** Number 19 serves Piazza del Risorgimento by way of San Lorenzo, Viale Regina Margherita and Villa Borghese.

Top Sights
Vatican Museums

Visiting the Vatican Museums is a thrilling and unforgettable experience. With some 7km of exhibitions and more masterpieces than many small countries can call their own, this vast museum complex boasts one of the world's greatest art collections. Highlights include a spectacular collection of classical statuary in the Museo Pio-Clementino, a suite of rooms frescoed by Raphael, and the Michelangelo-decorated Sistine Chapel.

👁 Map p140, C3

📞 06 6988 4676

www.museivaticani.va

Viale Vaticano

adult/reduced €16/8, last Sun of month free

🕘 9am-6pm Mon-Sat, 9am-2pm last Sun of month

Ⓜ Ottaviano-San Pietro

Sala Rotonda, Museo Pio-Clementino

Pinacoteca

Often overlooked by visitors, the papal picture gallery displays paintings dating from the 11th to 19th centuries, with works by Fra Angelico, Titian, Caravaggio and Leonardo da Vinci.

Museo Chiaramonti & Braccio Nuovo

This museum is effectively the long corridor that runs down the lower east side of the Palazzetto di Belvedere. Near the end of the hall, off to the right, is the **Braccio Nuovo** (New Wing), which contains a celebrated statue of the Nile as a reclining god covered by 16 babies.

Museo Pio-Clementino

To the left as you enter the **Cortile Ottagono** (Octagonal Courtyard) is the *Apollo Belvedere,* a 2nd-century Roman copy of a 4th-century-BC Greek bronze. A beautifully proportioned representation of the sun god Apollo, it's considered one of the great masterpieces of classical sculpture. Back inside, the **Sala degli Animali** is filled with sculpted creatures and some magnificent 4th-century mosaics.

Galleria delle Carte Geografiche

One of the unsung heroes of the Vatican Museums, the 120m-long Map Gallery is hung with 40 huge topographical maps. These were created between 1580 and 1583 for Pope Gregory XIII based on drafts by Ignazio Danti, one of the leading cartographers of his day.

Museo Gregoriano Egizio

Founded by Pope Gregory XVI in 1839, this Egyptian museum displays pieces taken from Egypt in ancient Roman times. The collection is small, but there are fascinating exhibits, including a fragmented statue of the pharaoh Ramses II on his throne, vividly painted sarcophagi dating from around 1000 BC, and a macabre mummy.

☑ **Top Tips**

▶ The museums are free on the last Sunday of the month.

▶ Exhibits are not well labelled, so consider hiring an audio guide (€7) or buying the *Guide to the Vatican Museums and City* (€14).

▶ To avoid queues book tickets online (http://biglietteriamusei.vatican.va/musei/tickets/do; plus €4 booking fee).

▶ Time your visit to minimise waiting: Tuesdays, Thursdays and Wednesday mornings are quietest; afternoon is better than morning; avoid Mondays when many other museums are shut.

✕ **Take a Break**

There's a self-service restaurant and cafe near the Pinacoteca, and a bar on the stairs to the Sistine Chapel.

For a real bite to remember, leave the museums and head to Pizzarium (p143), one of Rome's best *pizza al taglio* (sliced pizza) joints.

Vatican Museums

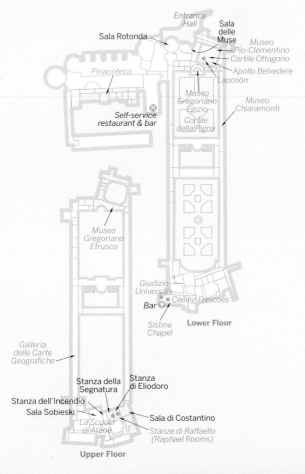

Entrance Hall

Sala delle Muse

Sala Rotonda

Museo Pio-Clementino

Cortile Ottagono

Apollo Belvedere

Laocoön

Pinacoteca

Museo Gregoriano Egizio

Museo Chiaramonti

Self-service restaurant & bar

Cortile della Pigna

Museo Gregoriano Etrusco

Giudizio Universale

Bar

Ceiling Frescoes

Lower Floor

Sistine Chapel

Galleria delle Carte Geografiche

Stanza della Segnatura

Stanza di Eliodoro

Stanza dell'Incendio

Sala Sobieski

Sala di Costantino

La Scuola di Atene

Stanze di Raffaello (Raphael Rooms)

Upper Floor

Frescoes by Raphael in the Stanza della Segnatura

Museo Gregoriano Etrusco

At the top of the 18th-century Simon-etti staircase, this fascinating museum contains artefacts unearthed in the Etruscan tombs of northern Lazio, as well as a superb collection of vases and Roman antiquities.

Stanze di Raffaello

These four frescoed chambers, currently undergoing partial restoration, were part of Pope Julius II's private apartments. Raphael himself painted the **Stanza della Segnatura** (1508–11) and the **Stanza d'Eliodoro** (1512–14), while the **Stanza dell'Incendio di Borgo** (1514–17) and **Sala di Costantino** (1517–24) were decorated by students following his designs.

Sistine Chapel – The Ceiling

The **Sistine Chapel** provided the greatest challenge of Michelangelo's career and painting the entire 800-sq-m vaulted ceiling at a height of more than 20m pushed him to the limits of his genius. Pope Julius II persuaded Michelangelo to accept the commission for a fee equivalent to between €1.5 and €2 million in today's money.

Sistine Chapel – Giudizio Universale

Michelangelo's second stint in the Sistine Chapel, from 1535 to 1541, resulted in the *Giudizio Universale* (Last Judgment), his highly charged depiction of Christ's second coming on the 200-sq-m western wall.

Top Sights
St Peter's Basilica

In a city of outstanding churches, none can hold a candle to St Peter's, Italy's largest, richest and most spectacular basilica. A monument to centuries of artistic genius, it boasts many spectacular works of art, including three of Italy's most celebrated masterpieces: Michelangelo's *Pietà*, his soaring dome, and Bernini's 29m-high baldachin over the papal altar.

The Dome
From the **dome** (with/without lift €8/6; ⊙8am-6pm summer, to 5pm winter; 🚇Piazza del Risorgimento,

⊙ Map p140, C4

☎ 06 6988 5518

www.vatican.va

St Peter's Square

admission free

⊙ 7am-7pm summer, to 6.30pm winter

Ⓜ Ottaviano-San Pietro

Statues of Jesus, John the Baptist and the apostles on the basilica's upper attic

Ⓜ Ottaviano-San Pietro) entrance on the right of the basilica's main portico, you can walk the 551 steps to the top or take a small lift halfway and then follow on foot for the last 320 steps. Either way, it's a long, steep climb. But make it to the top, and you're rewarded with stunning views from a perch 120m above St Peter's Square.

The Facade
Built between 1608 and 1612, Maderno's immense facade is 48m high and 115m wide. Eight 27m-high columns support the upper attic on which 13 statues stand representing Christ the Redeemer, St John the Baptist and the 11 apostles. The central balcony is known as the **Loggia della Benedizione**, and it's from here that the pope delivers his *Urbi et Orbi* blessing at Christmas and Easter.

Running across the entablature is an inscription that translates as 'In honour of the Prince of Apostles, Paul V Borghese, Roman, Pontiff, in the year 1612, the seventh of his pontificate'.

Interior – the Nave
Dominating the centre of the basilica is Bernini's 29m-high **baldachin**. Supported by four spiral columns and made with bronze taken from the Pantheon, it stands over the **papal altar**, also known as the Altar of the Confession. In front, Carlo Maderno's *Confessione* stands over the site where St Peter was originally buried.

Above the baldachin, Michelangelo's **dome** soars to a height of 119m. Based on Brunelleschi's design for the Duomo in Florence, it's supported by four massive stone piers, each named after the saint whose statue adorns its Bernini-designed niche. The saints are all associated with the basilica's four major relics: the lance St Longinus used to pierce Christ's side; the cloth with which St Veronica wiped Jesus' face; a fragment of the Cross collected by St Helena; and the head of St Andrew.

☑ Top Tips
▶ Dress appropriately if you want to get in – no shorts, miniskirts or bare shoulders.

▶ Between October and late May, free English-language tours of the basilica are run by seminarians from the Pontifical North American College. These generally start at 2.15pm Monday through Friday, leaving from the Ufficio Pellegrini e Turisti.

▶ Queues are inevitable at the security checks but they move quickly.

▶ Lines are generally shorter during lunch hours and late afternoon.

✕ Take a Break
Avoid the tourist traps around the basilica and head to nearby Prati where you'll find a wide choice of eateries. For a salad or tasty *panino* stop off at hit organic takeaway Fa-Bio (p143), while for something more substantial, join the fashionable neighbourhood diners at Il Sorpasso (p144).

At the base of the Pier of St Longinus is Arnolfo di Cambio's much-loved 13th-century bronze **statue of St Peter**, whose right foot has been worn down by centuries of caresses.

Behind the altar, the tribune is home to Bernini's extraordinary **Cattedra di San Pietro**. A vast gilded bronze throne held aloft by four 5m-high saints, it's centred on a wooden seat that was once thought to have been St Peter's but in fact dates to the 9th century.

Interior – Left Aisle

In the roped-off left transept, this **chapel** takes its name from the Madonna that stares out from Giacomo della Porta's marble altar. To its right, above the tomb of St Leo the Great,

is a fine relief by Alessandro Algardi. Under the next arch is Bernini's last work in the basilica, the **monument to Alexander VII**.

Halfway down the left aisle, the **Cappella Clementina** is named after Clement VIII, who had Giacomo della Porta decorate it for the Jubilee of 1600. Beneath the altar is the tomb of St Gregory the Great and, to the left, a monument to Pope Pius VII by Thorvaldsen.

The next arch shelters Alessandro Algardi's 16th-century monument to Leo XI. Beyond it, the richly decorated **Cappella del Coro** was created by Giovanni Battista Ricci to designs by Giacomo della Porta.

Continuing on, the **Cappella della Presentazione** contains two of the cathedral's most modern works: a

St Peter's Basilica

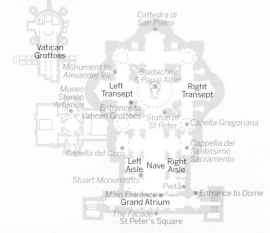

Cattedra di San Pietro

Vatican Grottoes

Monument to Alexander VII

Baldachin & Papal Altar

Museo Storico Artistico

Left Transept

Right Transept

Entrance to Vatican Grottoes

Statue of St Peter

Capella Gregoriana

Cappella del Coro

Cappella del Santissimo Sacramento

Left Aisle Nave Right Aisle

Stuart Monuments

Pietà

Entrance to Dome

Main Entrance

Grand Atrium

The Facade

St Peter's Square

Papal altar, featuring Bernini's baldachin (p137)

black relief monument to John XXIII by Emilio Greco, and a monument to Benedict XV by Pietro Canonica.

Located under the next arch are the **Stuart Monuments**; on the right is the monument to Clementina Sobieska, wife of James Stuart, by Filippo Barigioni, and on the left is Canova's vaguely erotic monument to the last three members of the Stuart clan, the pretenders to the English throne who died in exile in Rome.

Interior – Right Aisle

At the head of the right aisle is Michelangelo's hauntingly beautiful **Pietà**. Sculpted when he was only 25 (in 1499), it's the only work the artist ever signed – his signature is etched into the sash across the Madonna's breast.

Carlo Fontana's gilt and bronze monument to Queen Christina commemorates the far-from-holy Swedish monarch who converted to Catholicism in 1655.

Moving on, you'll come to the home of Pope John Paul II's tomb and a sumptuously decorated **baroque chapel** with works by Borromini, Bernini and Pietro da Cortona.

Beyond the chapel, a grandiose monument to Gregory XIII sits near the roped-off **Cappella Gregoriana**, a chapel built by Gregory XIII from designs by Michelangelo.

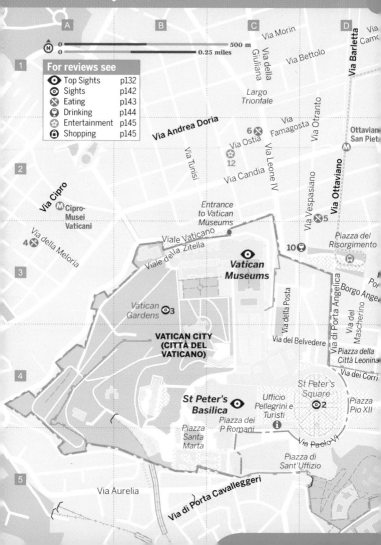

A   B   C   D

N 0 _____ 500 m
0 _____ 0.25 miles

For reviews see
- ◉ Top Sights   p132
- ◉ Sights   p142
- ✕ Eating   p143
- ☕ Drinking   p144
- ★ Entertainment   p145
- 🔒 Shopping   p145

Via Morin

Via della Giuliana

Via Bettolo

Via Barletta

Via Camo

Largo Trionfale

Via Andrea Doria

6 ✕ Via Famagosta

Via Ostia

Via Otranto

Via Leone IV

12 ★

Via Tunisi

Via Candia

Via Vespasiano

Ottaviani San Piet

Ⓜ

Via Ottaviano

5 ✕

Via Cipro Ⓜ Cipro-
Musei
Vaticani

Entrance to Vatican Museums

Piazza del Risorgimento

4 ✕ Via della Meloria

Viale Vaticano

10 ☕

Via di Porta Angelica

Borgo Ange

Viale della Zitella

◉ Vatican Museums

Via della Posta

Via del Mascherino

Por

Vatican Gardens ◉ 3

VATICAN CITY (CITTÀ DEL VATICANO)

Via del Belvedere

Piazza della Città Leonina

Via dei Corri

St Peter's Square

St Peter's Basilica ◉

Ufficio Pellegrini e Turisti ℹ

◉ 2

Piazza Pio XII

Piazza Santa Marta

Piazza dei P Romani

Via Paolo VI

Piazza di Sant'Uffizio

Via Aurelia

Via di Porta Cavalleggeri

Viale delle Milizie

Via Vigliena

Ponte
P Nenni

E

F

G

H

1

Via Damiata

Via Lepanto

Via Farnese

Lgt Michelangelo

Via C A
Dalla Chiesa

Lepanto Ⓜ

PRATI

Viale Giulio Cesare

Via degli Scipioni

Via Pompeo Magno

Ponte
Margherita

🎫9

Via Duilio

Via Ezio

Via Marcantonio Colonna

Via dei Gracchi

Piazza
della
Libertà

Via Caio Mario

Via Fabio Massimo

Piazza dei
Quiriti

2

🔒15

Via Emilio

Via A
Regolo

Via Germanico

14🚹

Via dei Gracchi

Via Cola di Rienzo

Via Valadier

Via Ennio
Quirini Visconti

Via Catullo

Via Plinio

Via Cicerone

Via Lucrezio Caro

Via Gioachino Belli

Lgt dei Mellini

Via
Varrone

13🎭

Via Propezio

Via Tibullo

Via Terenzio

Via Boezio

Via Orazio

Via Tacito

Via Muzio
Clementi

Via Pietro
Cossa

Via del Cavallini

3

Piazza
merigo
ipponi

🍴7

Via Cassiodoro

8🍴

Via Marianna
Dionigi

Via Crescenzio

Piazza
Cavour

Via Alberico II

Piazza Adriana

Via Tribuniano

Via Ulpiano

Lgt Prati

Via
Vitelleschi

Via Plauto

Via P
Castello

Largo di
Porta
Castello

Giardini di
Castel Sant'Angelo

Borgo Vittorio

Borgo Pio

Borgo Sant'Angelo

Castel
Sant'Angelo

🎯1

4

Piazza Pia

Lgt Castello

Ponte
Umberto I

Lgt Marzio

Via della Conciliazione

Via San
Pio X

Ponte Vittorio
Emanuele II

Lgt della
Altoviti

Ponte
Sant'Angelo

Tiber River

Piazza
Ponte
Umberto I

Lgt Tor di Nona

orgo Santo Spirito
Largo
Gregori

Lgt in Sassia

Lgt della
Fiorentini

Corso Vittorio
Emanuele II

Via dei Coronari

Via G
Zanardelli

Via del Banco di
Santo Spirito

5

Via di Porta
Santo Spirito

Ponte
Principe
Amedeo

Piazza
dell'Oro

Top Tip

See the Pope

Papal audiences are held at 10am on Wednesdays, usually in St Peter's Square but sometimes in the nearby Aula delle Udienze Pontificie Paolo VI (Paul VI Audience Hall). You'll need to book free tickets in advance. No tickets are required for the pope's Sunday blessing, at noon in St Peter's Square. See the Vatican website (www.vatican.va/various/prefettura/index_en.html) for more details.

Sights

Castel Sant'Angelo   MUSEUM, CASTLE

1 ◉ Map p140, F4

With its chunky round keep, this castle is an instantly recognisable landmark. Built as a mausoleum for the emperor Hadrian, it was converted into a papal fortress in the 6th century and named after an angelic vision that Pope Gregory the Great had in 590. Nowadays, it houses the Museo Nazionale di Castel Sant'Angelo and its eclectic collection of paintings, sculpture, military memorabilia and medieval firearms. (☏06 681 91 11; www.castelsantangelo.beniculturali.it; Lungotevere Castello 50; adult/reduced €10/5; ⊙9am-7.30pm, ticket office to 6.30pm; 🚌Piazza Pia)

St Peter's Square   PIAZZA

2 ◉ Map p140, D4

Overlooked by St Peter's Basilica, the Vatican's central square was laid out between 1656 and 1667 to a design by Gian Lorenzo Bernini. Seen from above, it resembles a giant keyhole with two semicircular colonnades, each consisting of four rows of Doric columns, encircling a giant ellipse that straightens out to funnel believers into the basilica. The effect was deliberate – Bernini described the colonnades as representing 'the motherly arms of the church'. (Piazza San Pietro; MOttaviano-San Pietro)

Vatican Gardens   GARDENS

3 ◉ Map p140

Up to a third of the Vatican is covered by the perfectly manicured Vatican Gardens, which contain fortifications, grottoes, monuments, fountains, and the state's tiny heliport. Visits are by two-hour guided tour only, for which you'll need to book at least a week in advance. Note that after the tour you're free to visit the Vatican Museums on your own. (www.museivaticani.va; adult/reduced incl Vatican Museums €32/24; ⊙by reservation only; 🚌Piazza del Risorgimento, MOttaviano-San Pietro)

Aerial view of the Vatican Gardens

Eating

Pizzarium
PIZZA €

4 Map p140, A3

When a pizza joint is packed at lunchtime on a wet winter's day, you know it's something special. Pizzarium, the takeaway of Gabriele Bonci, Rome's acclaimed pizza king, serves Rome's best sliced pizza, bar none. Scissor-cut squares of soft, springy base are topped with original combinations of seasonal ingredients and served on paper trays for immediate consumption. Also worth trying are the freshly fried *supplì* (crunchy rice croquettes). (☎06 3974 5416; Via della Meloria 43; pizza slices €5; ⏰11am-10pm; M Cipro-Musei Vaticani)

Fa-Bìo
SANDWICHES €

5 Map p140

Sandwiches, wraps, salads and fresh juices are all prepared with speed, skill and fresh organic ingredients at this friendly takeaway. Locals, Vatican tour guides and in-the-know visitors come here to grab a quick lunchtime bite and if you can find room in the tiny interior, you'd do well to follow suit. (☎06 6452 5810; www.fa-bio.com; Via Germanico 43; sandwiches €5; ⏰10.30am-5.30pm Mon-Fri, to 4pm Sat; 🚌 Piazza del Risorgimento, M Ottaviano-San Pietro)

Fatamorgana

GELATO €

6 Map p140

The Prati branch of hit gelateria chain, Fatamorgana. As well as all the classic flavours there are some wonderfully left-field creations, including a strange but delicious *basilico, miele e noci* (basil, honey and hazelnuts). (www.gelateriafatamorgana.it; Via Leone IV 52; gelato €2.50-5; ⏱noon-11pm summer, to 9pm winter; ⓜOttaviano-San Pietro)

Il Sorpasso

ITALIAN €€

7 Map p140, E3

A bar-restaurant hybrid sporting a vintage cool look – vaulted stone ceilings, exposed brick, rustic wooden tables – Il Sorpasso is a Prati hotspot. Open throughout the day, it caters to a fashionable crowd, serving everything from salads and pasta specials to *trappizini* (pyramids of stuffed pizza), cured meats and cocktails. (☎06 8902 4554; www.sorpasso.info; Via Properzio 31-33; meals €20-35; ⏱7am-1am Mon-Fri, 9am-1am Sat; 🚇Piazza del Risorgimento)

Ristorante L'Arcangelo

RISTORANTE €€€

8 Map p140, G3

Styled as an informal bistro with wood panelling, leather banquettes and casual table settings, L'Arcangelo enjoys a stellar local reputation. Dishes are modern and creative yet still undeniably Roman in their use of traditional ingredients such as sweetbreads and *baccalà* (cod). A further plus is the wine list, which boasts some interesting Italian labels. (☎06 321 09 92; www.larcangelo.com; Via Giuseppe G Belli 59; meals €50; ⏱1-2.30pm Mon-Fri & 8-11pm Mon-Sat; 🚇Piazza Cavour)

Drinking

Sciascia Caffè

CAFE

9 Map p140, E2

There are several contenders for the best coffee in town but in our opinion, nothing tops the *caffè eccellente* served at this polished old-school cafe. A velvety smooth espresso served in a delicate cup lined with melted chocolate, it's nothing short of magnificent. (☎06 321 15 80; Via Fabio Massimo 80/A; ⏱7am-8.30pm Mon-Sat, 8am-8pm Sun; ⓜOttaviano-San Pietro)

Be.re

CRAFT BEER

10 Map p140

Rome's craft-beer fans keenly applauded the opening of this contemporary bar in late 2016. With its copper beer taps, exposed brick decor and high vaulted ceilings, it's a good-looking spot for an evening of Italian beers and cask ales. And should hunger strike, there's a branch of hit takeaway Trappizino right next door. (☎06 9442 1854; www.be-re.eu; Piazza del Risorgimento, cnr Via Vespasiano; ⏱10am-2am; 🚇Piazza del Risorgimento)

Makasar Bistrot   WINE BAR, TEAHOUSE

11 🖳 Map p140, E4

Recharge your batteries with a quiet drink at this bookish *bistrot*. Pick your tipple from the 250-variety tea menu or opt for an Italian wine and sit back in the softly lit earthenware-hued interior. For something to eat, there's a small menu of salads, bruschetta, baguettes and hot dishes. (📞06 687 46 02; www.makasar.it; Via Plauto 33; ⏰noon-midnight Mon-Thu, to 2am Fri & Sat, 5pm-midnight Sun; 🚇Piazza del Risorgimento)

Entertainment

Alexanderplatz   JAZZ

12 ⭐ Map p140, C2

Intimate, underground, and hard to find – look for the discreet black door – Rome's most celebrated jazz club draws top Italian and international performers and a respectful cosmopolitan crowd. Book a table for the best stage views or to dine here, although note that it's the music that's the star act, not the food. (📞06 8377 5604; www.facebook.com/alexander.platz.37; Via Ostia 9; ⏰8.30pm-1.30am; Ⓜ️Ottaviano-San Pietro)

Fonclea   LIVE MUSIC

13 ⭐ Map p140, E3

Fonclea is a great little pub venue, with nightly gigs by bands playing everything from jazz and soul to pop, rock and doo-wop. Get in the mood with a drink during happy hour (6pm to 8.30pm daily). In summer, the pub ups sticks and moves to a site by the Tiber. (📞06 689 63 02; www.fonclea.it; Via Crescenzio 82a; ⏰6pm-2am Sep-May, concerts 9.30pm; 🚇Piazza del Risorgimento)

Shopping

Rechicle   VINTAGE

14 🔒 Map p140

Lovers of vintage fashions should make a beeline for this fab boutique. Furnished with antique family furniture and restored cabinets, it's full of wonderful finds such as Roger Vivier comma heels (with their original box), iconic Chanel jackets, Hermès bags, Balenciaga coats and much more besides. (📞06 3265 2469; Piazza dell' Unità 21; ⏰10.30am-2pm & 3.30-7.30pm Mon-Sat; 🚇Via Cola di Rienzo)

Il Sellaio   FASHION & ACCESSORIES

15 🔒 Map p140

During the 1960s Ferruccio Serafini was one of Rome's most sought-after artisans, making handmade leather shoes and bags for the likes of JFK, Liz Taylor and Marlon Brando. Nowadays, his daughter Francesca runs the family shop where you can pick up beautiful hand-stitched bags, belts and accessories. You can also have your own designs made to order. (📞06 321 17 19; www.serafinipelletteria.it; Via Caio Mario 14; ⏰9.30am-7.30pm Mon-Fri, 9.30am-1pm & 3.30-7.30pm Sat; Ⓜ️Ottaviano-San Pietro)

Top Sights
Villa Borghese

Getting There

🚌 Take bus 53 or 910 to Via Pinciana.

Ⓜ From Spagna you can walk up to Villa Borghese via a long series of elevators and underground passageways.

Locals, lovers, tourists, joggers – no one can resist the lure of Rome's most celebrated park. Originally the 17th-century estate of Cardinal Scipione Borghese, it covers about 80 hectares of wooded glades, gardens and grassy banks. Among its attractions are several excellent museums, the landscaped Giardino del Lago, Piazza di Siena, a dusty arena used for Rome's top equestrian event in May, and a panoramic terrace on the Pincio Hill.

Museo e Galleria Borghese

Museo e Galleria Borghese

If you only have the time (or inclination) for one art gallery in Rome, make it the **Museo e Galleria Borghese** (📞 06 3 28 10; www.galleriaborghese.it; Piazzale del Museo Borghese 5; adult/reduced €15/8.50; 🕙9am-7pm Tue-Sun; 🚌Via Pinciana). Housing what's often referred to as the 'queen of all private art collections', it boasts paintings by Caravaggio, Raphael, and Titian, as well as some sensational sculptures by Bernini. Highlights abound, but look out for Bernini's *Ratto di Proserpina* (Rape of Proserpina) and Canova's *Venere vincitrice* (Venus Victrix).

The museum's collection was formed by Cardinal Scipione Borghese (1579–1633), the most knowledgeable and ruthless art collector of his day. It was originally housed in the cardinal's residence near St Peter's but in the 1620s he had it transferred to his new villa just outside Porta Pinciana. And it's here, in the villa's central building, the Casino Borghese, that you'll see it today.

To limit numbers, visitors are admitted at two-hourly intervals, so you'll need to pre-book your ticket and get an entry time.

Museo Nazionale Etrusco di Villa Giulia

Pope Julius III's 16th-century **villa** (📞 06 322 65 71; www.villagiulia.beniculturali.it; Piazzale di Villa Giulia; adult/reduced €8/4; 🕙8.30am-7.30pm Tue-Sun; 🚌Via delle Belle Arti) provides the charming setting for Italy's finest collection of Etruscan and pre-Roman treasures. Exhibits, many of which came from tombs in the surrounding Lazio region, range from bronze figurines and black *bucchero* tableware to temple decorations, terracotta vases and dazzling jewellery.

Perhaps the museum's most famous piece is the 6th-century BC *Sarcofago degli Sposi* (Sarcophagus of the Betrothed). This astonishing work,

---

www.sovraintendenza
roma.it

entrances at Piazzale San Paolo del Brasile, Piazzale Flaminio, Via Pinciana, Via Raimondo, Largo Pablo Picasso

🕙sunrise-sunset

🚌Via Pinciana

☑ Top Tips

▶ Admission to the Museo e Galleria Borghese is free on the first Sunday of the month.

▶ Bike hire is available at various points, including Largo Pablo Picasso, for €5/15 per hour/day.

✕ Take a Break

For a relaxing drink or romantic meal, head to **Caffè delle Arti** (📞 06 3265 1236; www.caffedelleartiroma.com; Via Gramsci 73; meals €40-45; 🕙8am-5pm Mon, 8am-midnight Tue-Sun; 🚌Piazza Thorvaldsen), located in La Galleria Nazionale.

Further away, the **Osteria Flaminio** (📞 06 323 69 00; www.osteriaflaminio.com; Via Flaminia 297; lunch buffet €8-12; 🕙12.30-3.30pm & 7.30pm-midnight; 🚌Via Flaminia) is popular for its bargain buffet lunch.

originally unearthed in a tomb in Cerveteri, depicts a husband and wife reclining on a stone banqueting couch. And although called a sarcophagus, it was actually designed as an elaborate urn for the couple's ashes.

Museo Carlo Bilotti

The Orangery of Villa Borghese provides the handsome setting for the **art collection** (☑ 06 06 08; www.museocarlo bilotti.it; Viale Fiorello La Guardia; admission free; ⏱ 10am-4pm Tue-Fri, 10am-7pm Sat & Sun winter, 1-7pm Tue-Fri, 10am-7pm Sat & Sun summer; ☐ Via Pinciana) of billionaire cosmetics magnate Carlo Bilotti. The main focus is 18 works by Giorgio de Chirico (1888–1978), one of Italy's foremost modern artists, but also of note is a Warhol portrait of Bilotti's wife and daughter.

Giardino del Lago

Designed and laid out in the late 18th century, this leafy area is centred on a small, romantic **lake** (Villa Borghese; boat hire per 20min €3; ⏱ 7am-9pm summer, to 6pm winter; ☐ Via Pinciana). The highlight, other than the serene atmosphere, is the Tempietto di Esculapio, a copy of a Roman temple sited on the lake's artificial islet.

Nearby: La Galleria Nazionale

Housed in a vast belle-époque palace, this oft-overlooked modern **art gallery** (☑ 06 3229 8221; http://lagallerianazionale. com; Viale delle Belle Arti 131, accessible entrance Via Antonio Gramsci 71; adult/reduced €10/5; ⏱ 8.30am-7.30pm Tue-Sun; ☐ Piazza Thorvaldsen), known locally as GNAM, is an unsung gem. Its superlative collection runs the gamut from neoclassical sculpture to abstract expressionism with works by many of the most important exponents of 19th- and 20th-century art.

Nearby: Museo Nazionale delle Arti del XXI Secolo

As much as the exhibitions, the highlight of Rome's leading contemporary **art gallery** (MAXXI; ☑ 06 320 19 54; www. fondazionemaxxi.it; Via Guido Reni 4a; adult/reduced €12/8, permanent collection free Tue-Fri & 1st Sun of month; ⏱ 11am-7pm Tue-Fri & Sun, to 10pm Sat; ☐ Viale Tiziano) is the Zaha Hadid–designed building it occupies. Formerly a barracks, the curved concrete structure is striking inside and out with a multilayered geometric facade and a cavernous light-filled interior full of snaking walkways and suspended staircases. The gallery has a permanent collection of 20th- and 21st-century works, but more interesting are its international exhibitions.

Nearby: Auditorium Parco della Musica

The hub of Rome's thriving cultural scene, the **Auditorium** (☑ 06 8024 1281; www.auditorium.com; Viale Pietro de Coubertin; ☐ Viale Tiziano) is the capital's premier concert venue. Its three concert halls and 3000-seat open-air arena stage everything from classical music concerts to jazz gigs, public lectures and film screenings.

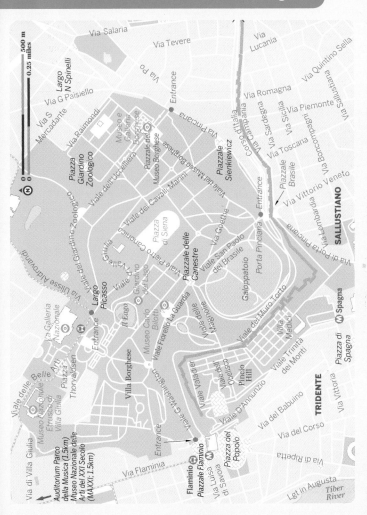

VRBANVS VIII PONT MAX
AMBVLATIONIS GREGORIANAE
FVNDAMENTVM A QVAE SVBLAPSVS NO LA
PARIETE SE PORNICE AD IMBRIVM ET TEMPORIS INIVRIA VINDICAVIT
PICTVRAS IN DIES PAENE DESOLE SCENTES INSTAVRAVIT
GEO GRADAM ANVLIS INLOCIS C ORR EXIT PAVIT
VNDE SA QVEVT AR VMEC TVM LVS
EDINO DECOR EDITVITAG MDCXXXVII ANNO III

GENVA
MARITIMAM IVVENTV QVT
VANALI MOTISII VDTTIO
CLARVM SARTOR
SPORT INTERATIS
IN DTA
MVNDISTMVMS SVPER
IMPETICIADE MANVBV A
IVSTIA
CLARISSIMAE RISPVBLICAE
OLI PRAEBET

The Best of
Rome

Rome's Best Walks

Rome's Best...

Galleria delle Carte Geografiche (p133), Vatican Museums
BRIAN KINNEY/SHUTTERSTOCK ©

Best Walks
Emperor's Footsteps

🏃 The Walk

Follow in the footsteps of Rome's legendary emperors on this walk around the best of the city's ancient treasures. Established in 27 BC, the Roman Empire grew to become the Western world's first dominant superpower and at the peak of its power, in about AD 100, it extended from Britain to north Africa, and from Syria to Spain. Rome had a population of more than 1.5 million and all of the trappings of imperial splendour: marble temples, public baths, theatres, shopping centres and, of course, the Colosseum.

Start Colosseum; Ⓜ Colosseo

Finish Vittoriano; 🚊 Piazza Venezia

Length 2km; at least three hours

✕ Take a Break

Hidden away in the Capitoline Museums but accessible by its own entrance, the **Terrazza Caffarelli** (p34) is a refined spot for a restorative coffee.

BELT944-SHUTTERSTOCK ©

Vittoriano (p33)

❶ Colosseum

More than any other monument, it's the **Colosseum** (p24) that symbolises the power and glory of ancient Rome. A spectacular feat of engineering, the 50,000-seat stadium was inaugurated by Emperor Titus in AD80 with a bloodthirsty bout of games that lasted 100 days and nights.

❷ Palatino

A short walk from the Colosseum, the **Palatino** (p31) was ancient Rome's most sought-after neighbourhood, site of the emperor's palace and home to the cream of imperial society. The evocative ruins are confusing but their grandeur gives some sense of the luxury in which the ancient VIPs liked to live.

❸ Roman Forum

Coming down from the Palatino you'll enter the **Roman Forum** (p26) near the Arco di Tito, one of Rome's great triumphal arches. In imperial times, the Forum was the empire's nerve centre, a teeming hive of law courts, temples, piazzas and shops. The vestal virgins lived here and senators debated matters of state in the **Curia** (p27).

④ Piazza del Campidoglio

Exit the Forum onto Via dei Fori Imperiali and head up to the Michelangelo-designed **Piazza del Campidoglio** (p32). This striking piazza, one of Rome's most beautiful, sits atop the Campidoglio (Capitoline hill), one of the seven hills on which

Rome was founded. In ancient times this was the spiritual heart of the city, home to two of the city's most important temples.

⑤ Capitoline Museums

Flanking Piazza del Campidoglio are two stately *palazzi* (mansions) that together house the **Capitoline Museums** (p32). These, the world's oldest public museums, boast an important picture gallery and a superb collection of classical sculpture

that includes an iconic Etruscan bronze, the *Lupa Capitolina*, of a wolf standing over Romulus and Remus.

⑥ Vittoriano

From the Campidoglio, pop next door to the massive mountain of white marble that is the **Vittoriano** (p33). No emperor ever walked here, but it's worth stopping off to take the panoramic lift to the top, from where you can see the whole of Rome laid out beneath you.

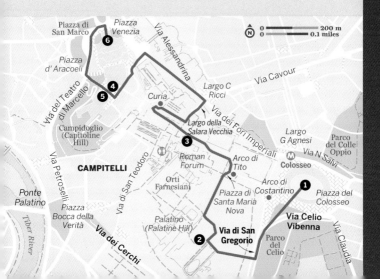

Best Walks
Piazzas of Rome

🏃 The Walk

Rome's tightly packed historic centre boasts some of the city's most celebrated piazzas, and several beautiful but lesser known squares. Each has its own character – the baroque splendour of Piazza Navona, the bawdy clamour of Campo de' Fiori, the Renaissance elegance of Piazza Farnese – but together they encapsulate much of the city's beauty, history and drama. Take this tour to discover the best of them and enjoy the area's vibrant street life.

Start Largo di Torre Argentina; 🚃 Largo di Torre Argentina

Finish Piazza Farnese; 🚃 Corso Vittorio Emanuele II

Length 1.5km; three hours

🍴 Take a Break

Between the Pantheon and Piazza Navona, **Caffè Sant'Eustachio** (p49) is a good bet for a quick pit stop. Its coffee is reckoned by many to be the best in Rome.

Piazza Navona (p44)

TROTALO/SHUTTERSTOCK ©

❶ Largo di Torre Argentina

Start off in **Largo di Torre Argentina**, set around the ruins of four Republic-era temples. On the piazza's western flank, the **Teatro Argentina** (p51), Rome's premier theatre, sits near the site where Julius Caesar was assassinated.

❷ Piazza della Minerva

Head along Via dei Cestari until you come to Piazza della Minerva and the Elefantino, a sculpture of a puzzled elephant carrying an Egyptian obelisk. Flanking the square, the Gothic **Basilica di Santa Maria Sopra Minerva** (p45) boasts Renaissance frescoes and a minor Michelangelo.

❸ Piazza di Sant'Ignazio Loyola

Strike off down Via Santa Caterina da Siena, then take Via del Pièdi Marmo and Via di Sant'Ignazio to reach the exquisite 18th-century **Piazza di Sant'Ignazio Loyola**. Overlooking the piazza, the Chiesa di Sant'Ignazio di Loyola features a magical trompe l'oeil ceiling fresco.

❹ Piazza della Rotonda

A short stroll down Via del Seminario brings you to the bustling **Piazza della Rotonda**, where the **Pantheon** (p38) needs no introduction. Rome's best-preserved ancient building is one of the city's iconic sights with its epic portico and dome.

❺ Piazza Navona

From the Pantheon, follow the signs to **Piazza Navona** (p44), central Rome's great showpiece square. Here, among the street artists, tourists and pigeons, you can compare the two giants of Roman baroque – Gian Lorenzo Bernini, creator of the Fontana dei Quattro Fiumi, and Francesco Borromini, author of the Chiesa di Sant'Agnese in Agone.

❻ Campo de' Fiori

On the other side of Corso Vittorio Emanuele II, the busy road that bisects the *centro storico* (historic centre), life is focused on **Campo de' Fiori** (p51). By day, this noisy square stages a colourful market, at night it transforms into a raucous open-air pub.

❼ Piazza Farnese

Just beyond the Campo, **Piazza Farnese** is a refined square overlooked by the Renaissance **Palazzo Farnese** (p46). This magnificent *palazzo* (mansion), now home to the French embassy, boasts some superb frescoes, said by some to rival those of the Sistine Chapel.

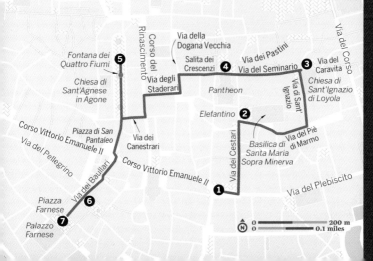

Best
History

For thousands of years Rome was at the centre of world events. First, as *caput mundi* (capital of the world), the glittering hub of the vast Roman Empire, and then as the seat of papal power. It was a city that counted – and this is writ large on its historic streets, where every *palazzo,* church and ancient ruin has a tale to tell.

ARQGANT/SHUTTERSTOCK ©

Ancient Glories

Many of Rome's most thrilling monuments hark back to its golden age as capital of the mighty Roman Empire. The Colosseum, the Pantheon, the Roman Forum – these epic ruins all tell of past glories in a way that no textbook ever can, evoking images of teeming crowds and gladiatorial combat, pagan ceremonies and daily drama.

The Church Rules

For much of its history, the Church called the shots in Rome and many of the city's top sights are religious in origin. Early basilicas stand testament to the tenacity of the Church's founding fathers, while the masterpieces that litter the city's churches testify to the wealth and ambition of the Renaissance and baroque popes.

Multilayered History

One of Rome's characteristic features is the way that history quite literally rises from the ground. Over the centuries the city has undergone several transformations and with each one a new layer was added to the city's urban fabric. As a result, medieval churches stand over pagan temples and baroque piazzas sit atop Roman arenas. In Rome, to travel back in time you merely have to go underground.

Best Roman Relics

Colosseum Rome's iconic arena embodies all the drama of the ancient city. (p24)

Pantheon This awe-inspiring building has served as an architectural blueprint for millenniums. (p38)

Roman Forum The inspiring ruins of ancient Rome's bustling city centre. (p26)

Palatino Ancient emperors languished in luxury on the Palatino, imperial Rome's oldest and most exclusive neighbourhood. (p31)

Terme di Caracalla The towering remains of this ancient leisure centre are among Rome's most impressive. (p111)

Best Underground History

Basilica di San Clemente This medieval basilica sits over a pagan temple and 1st-century house. (p101)

Catacombs The Via Appia Antica (Appian Way) is riddled with catacombs where the early Christians buried their dead. (p93)

Case Romane Head underground to explore the houses where apostles John and Paul supposedly lived. (p102)

Best Historical Churches

St Peter's Basilica The Vatican's monumental showpiece church stands over St Peter's tomb. (p136)

Basilica di San Giovanni in Laterano The main papal basilica until the 14th century. (p98)

Basilica di San Paolo Fuori le Mura Monumental basilica on the site where St Paul was buried. (p107)

Chiesa del Gesù Important Jesuit church, home to Ignatius Loyola for 12 years. (p44)

Best for Legends

Palatino Where the wolf saved Romulus and Remus, and Rome was founded in 753 BC. (p31)

Bocca della Verità Tell a lie and the 'Mouth of Truth' will bite your hand off. (p33)

Basilica di San Pietro in Vincoli Houses the miraculous chains that bound St Peter. (p86)

Trevi Fountain Throw a coin in and you'll return to Rome. (p68)

Teatro Argentina Rome's top theatre overlooks the site where Julius Caesar was assassinated. (p51)

Basilica di Santa Maria del Popolo Was supposedly built to exorcise Nero's malicious spirit, which haunted the area. (p59)

Worth a Trip

Rome's answer to Pompeii, the **Scavi Archeologici di Ostia Antica** (📞06 5635 0215; www.ostiaantica.beniculturali.it; Viale dei Romagnoli 717; adult/reduced €8/4, free 1st Sun of month, exhibitions €3; ⏱8.30am-6.15pm Tue-Sun summer, shorter hours winter) offer a well-preserved insight into ancient Rome's once-thriving port. Highlights include the Terme di Nettuno and the impressive amphitheatre. To get there, take the suburban train to Ostia Antica from Stazione Porta San Paolo next to Piramide metro station.

Best
Food

Food is central to the Roman passion for life. Everyone has an opinion on it and the city teems with trattorias, pizzerias, fine-dining restaurants and gourmet gelaterie. Traditional Roman cooking holds sway but *cucina creativa* (creative cooking) has taken off in recent years and there are plenty of exciting, contemporary restaurants to try.

SUSAN WRIGHT/LONELY PLANET ©

The Traditional Trattoria

The bedrock of the Roman food scene has always been the family-run trattorias that pepper the city's streets and piazzas. These simple eateries, often with rickety wooden tables and *nonna* (grandma) at the stove, have been feeding visitors for centuries and are still the best bet for hearty, no-nonsense Roman dishes such as *bucatini all'amatriciana* (thick spaghetti with tomato sauce and *guanciale* – cured pig's cheek) or spaghetti *alla gricia* (with pancetta and *pecorino* – sheep's milk cheese).

Contemporary Fine Dining

Over recent decades Rome's restaurant scene has become increasingly sophisticated with new-wave trattorias and chic designer restaurants offering edgy, innovative food. Leading the way, Cristina Bowerman of Romeo e Giulietta and Giuseppe Di Iorio of Aroma have made their names with their modern, creative approach to Italian cuisine.

Street Food

The latest foodie fad to hit Rome is a passion for street food. Alongside the many *pizza al taglio* (sliced pizza) joints and gelaterie, a host of hip new places have opened across town serving classic snacks such as *supplì* (fried rice balls with various fillings) and *fritti* (fried foods) with a modern twist.

☑ **Top Tips**

▶ In a trattoria or restaurant, you'll be given bread and charged for it whether you eat it or not. This is standard practice, not a tourist rip-off.

▶ For water, ask for *acqua naturale* (still) or *acqua frizzante* (sparkling).

▶ Round the bill up in a pizzeria or trattoria in lieu of a tip; leave up to 10% in a more upmarket restaurant.

Italian cuisine

Best Fine Dining

Antonello Colonna Open Chef Antonello Colonna's glass-roofed restaurant offers creative takes on Roman classics. (p87)

Aroma Beautiful setting, and chef Giuseppe Di Iorio bedazzles with forward-thinking Mediterranean cuisine. (p103)

Imàgo Haute cuisine and haute views from the rooftop restaurant of the five-star Hassler Hotel. (p61)

Best Traditional Roman

Flavio al Velavevodetto Classic *cucina romana*, served in huge portions. (p113)

Da Felice In the heartland of Roman cuisine, and sticking to a traditional weekly timetable. (p113)

Armando al Pantheon Family-run trattoria offering hearty Roman cuisine in the shadow of the Pantheon. (p48)

Da Enzo Hugely popular Trastevere address, known for quality sourced ingredients. (p125)

Da Augusto Dreamy summertime dining and fabulous mamma-style cooking on one of Trastevere's prettiest piazzas. (p121)

Best Fast Food

Trapizzino Home of the *trapizzino*, a cone of doughy bread with fillers like *polpette al sugo* (meatballs in tomato sauce). (p113)

Mercato Centrale The hot spot at Rome's central train station for gourmet food fast. (p88)

Fa-Bìo Popular organic takeaway near the Vatican. (p143)

Mordi e Vai Classic Roman street food at this acclaimed Testaccio food stall. (p113)

Pasta Chef Fast pasta at a trendy 'gourmet street food' address in Monti. (p88)

Best Gelato

Fatamorgana Rome's finest artisanal flavours, now in multiple central locations. (p144)

Gelateria del Teatro Around 40 choices of delicious ice cream, all made on site. (p48)

Fior di Luna Great artisan ice cream in Trastevere. (p125)

Best
For Free

Rome is an expensive city, but you don't have to break the bank to enjoy it. A surprising number of its big sights are free and it costs nothing to stroll the historic streets, piazzas and parks, basking in their extraordinary beauty.

EMPEROROSSAR/SHUTTERSTOCK ©

Best Places for Free Art

St Peter's Basilica Michelangelo's *Pieta* is just one of the masterpieces on display. (p136)

Basilica di San Pietro in Vincoli Feast your eyes on Michelangelo's fearsome *Moses*. (p86)

Chiesa di San Luigi dei Francesi Caravaggio's St Matthew cycle is the big drawcard here. (p45)

Chiesa di Santa Maria della Vittoria Features Bernini's astonishing *Ecstasy of St Teresa*, a seminal baroque work. (p73)

Vatican Museums Free on the last Sunday of the month. (p132)

Best Piazzas & Parks

Piazza Navona A colourful cast of street artists create a carnival atmosphere on this stunning baroque piazza. (p44)

Campo de' Fiori Revel in the chaos of the Campo's daily market. (p51)

Piazza di Spagna People watch and mingle with other travellers in this iconic piazza. (p56)

Villa Borghese Rome's central park is ideal for leisurely strolling and picnics. (p147)

Gianicolo Admire magnificent views from this leafy hill. (p124)

Best Free Monuments

Pantheon It doesn't cost a penny to enter this extraordinary church. (p38)

Trevi Fountain Free, unless you thrown in a coin to ensure your return to Rome. (p68)

☑ Top Tips

▶ All state-run museums and sites are free on the first Sunday of the month.

▶ Save a few euros by filling up with water from drinking fountains known as *nasoni* (big noses) dotted around the streets.

Bocca della Verità Test the legend – tell a lie with your hand in the mouth. (p33; pictured above)

Spanish Steps Grab a perch and hang out on Rome's most celebrated staircase. (p56)

Best
Bars & Nightlife

Often the best way to enjoy nightlife in Rome is to wander from restaurant to bar, getting happily lost down picturesque cobbled streets. There's simply no city with better backdrops for a drink: you can savour a Campari overlooking the Roman Forum or sample some artisanal beer while watching the light bounce off baroque fountains.

NICK_NICK/SHUTTERSTOCK ©

Best Areas

Centro Storico Bars and a few clubs, a mix of touristy and sophisticated. (p49)

Trastevere Everyone's favourite place for a *passeggiata* (evening stroll), with plenty of bars and cafes. (p126)

Testaccio With a cluster of mainstream clubs, this nightlife strip offers poptastic choice. (p114)

Ostiense Home to Rome's cooler nightclubs, housed in ex-industrial venues. (p106)

San Lorenzo & Pigneto Favoured by students, with a concentration of bars and alternative clubs. (p78)

Best Wine Bars

Il Sorì Gourmet wine bar and artisan *bottegha* (shop) with wine tastings

and 'meet the producer' soirées. (p79)

Bibenda Wine Concept Modern wine bar with a good choice of regional Italian labels. (p104)

Ai Tre Scalini Buzzing *enoteca* that feels as convivial as a pub. (p87)

Best Aperitivo

Freni e Frizioni Perenially cool bar with lavish nightly buffet of snacks. (p121)

Doppiozeroo Popular Ostiense address with impressive buffet choice. (p107)

Pimm's Good Pimms cocktails, generous complimentary nibbles and party-loving bar staff in Trastevere. (p126)

Zuma Bar When the urge for a posh cocktail on a designer rooftop beckons. (p63)

☑ **Top Tip**

▶ Romans tend to dress up to go out, particularly in the smarter clubs and bars in the *centro storico* and Testaccio. However, over in Pigneto and San Lorenzo the style is much more alternative.

Best Clubs

Circolo Illuminati Wildly popular Ostiense club on the international DJ club circuit, with an underground vibe and star-topped courtyard. (p107)

Vinile Food, music, dancing and party happenings on the southern fringe of Ostiense. (p107)

Best
Architecture

Boasting ancient ruins, Renaissance basilicas, baroque churches and hulking fascist *palazzi*, Rome's architectural legacy is unparalleled. Michelangelo, Bramante, Borromini and Berniniare among the architects who have stamped their genius on its remarkable city scape, while in recent times a number of the world's top architects have completed projects in the city.

Ancient Engineering

In building the *caput mundi* (capital of the world), ancient Rome's architects and engineers were called on to design houses, roads, aqueducts and shopping centres alongside temples, tombs and imperial palaces. To do so they advanced methods devised by the Etruscans and Greeks and developed construction techniques that allowed them to build on a hitherto unseen scale.

Renaissance & Baroque Makeovers

Many of Rome's great *palazzi* and basilicas date to the Renaissance 16th century, including St Peter's Basilica, which was given a complete overhaul by Bramante, Michelangelo et al. A century later, the Counter-Reformation paved the way for a Church-sponsored makeover led by the baroque heroes Gian Lorenzo Bernini and Francesco Borromini.

Modern Architecture

In the early 20th century, Italy's Fascist dictator Benito Mussolini oversaw a number of grandiose building projects, including Via dei Fori Imperiali and the EUR district. More recently, projects have been completed by a roll-call of top international 'starchitects' including Renzo Piano, Massimiliano Fuksas, Richard Meier and Zaha Hadid.

Best Ancient Monuments

Colosseum A blueprint for modern stadiums, Rome's gladiatorial arena dramatically illustrates the use of the arch. (p24)

Pantheon The ancient Romans' greatest architectural achievement was revolutionary in both design and execution. (p38)

Terme di Caracalla These looming ruins hint at the sophistication of ancient building techniques. (p111)

Mercati di Traiano Museo dei Fori Imperiali A towering model of 2nd-century civic engineering. (p32)

Best Early Basilicas

Basilica di San Giovanni in Laterano Its original design set the

St Peter's Basilica (p136), Vatican City

style for basilicas to follow. (p98)

Basilica di Santa Maria Maggiore The only one of Rome's four patriarchal basilicas to retain its original layout. (p85)

Basilica di Santa Sabina This medieval gem sports an austere, no-frills basilica look. (p112)

Basilica di Santa Maria in Trastevere Ancient Roman columns and glittering mosaics feature in this Trastevere highlight. (p118)

Best Renaissance Buildings

St Peter's Basilica An amalgamation of designs, styles and plans, capped by Michelangelo's extraordinary dome. (p136)

Palazzo Farnese Home to the French embassy, this is a fine example of a Renaissance palace. (p46)

Piazza del Campidoglio Michelangelo's hilltop piazza is a show-stopping model of Renaissance town planning. (p32)

Best Baroque Gems

St Peter's Square Bernini designed the Vatican's focal square to funnel believers into St Peter's Basilica. (p142)

Piazza Navona With a Borromini church and a Bernini fountain, this square is a model of baroque beauty. (p44)

Best Modern Icons

Auditorium Parco della Musica Renzo Piano's avant-garde concert complex features a unique architectural design. (p148)

Museo dell'Ara Pacis Controversially designed by Richard Meier, this white pavilion houses an important 1st-century-BC altar. (p60; pictured above left)

Museo Nazionale delle Arti del XXI Secolo Zaha Hadid's converted barracks houses Rome's top contemporary art museum. (p148)

Best
Art & Museums

Home to some of the Western world's greatest art, Rome is a visual feast. Its churches contain more masterpieces than many small countries and its museums and galleries are laden with instantly recognisable works. From classical statues and stunning Renaissance frescoes to breathtaking baroque sculptures and futuristic paintings, the art on show spans almost 3000 years of artistic endeavour.

VALERIOMEI/SHUTTERSTOCK ©

Classical Art

Not surprisingly, Rome's collection of ancient art – largely comprising sculpture, commemorative reliefs, and mosaics – is unparalleled. The Vatican Museums and Capitoline Museums showcase much of the city's finest classical sculpture, but you'll also find superlative pieces in Palazzo Altemps and Palazzo Massimo alle Terme.

The Renaissance

The Renaissance unleashed an artistic maelstrom in Rome as powerful Church patrons commissioned artists such as Michelangelo and Raphael to decorate the city's basilicas and palaces. Fresco painting was a key endeavour and many celebrated frescoes date to this period, including Michelangelo's Sistine Chapel designs (in the Vatican Museums).

The Baroque

The baroque burst onto Rome's art scene in the early 17th century and was enthusiastically adopted by the Church as a propaganda tool in its battle against Reformation heresy. Works by the period's two leading artists – Gian Lorenzo Bernini and controversial painter Caravaggio – adorn churches and museums across the city.

☑ Top Tips

▶ Most museums are closed on Mondays.

▶ EU citizens under 18 years often qualify for free admission. Take ID as proof of age.

▶ Many museums close their ticket offices up to 75 minutes before closing time.

Modern Art

The 20th century saw the emergence of futurism, a nationalistic modernist movement, and metaphysical painting, an Italian form of surrealism best expressed in the works of Giorgio de Chirico.

Best Museums & Galleries

Vatican Museums
The Sistine Chapel and Raphael Rooms headline at this spectacular museum complex. (p132)

Museo e Galleria Borghese Houses Rome's best baroque sculpture and some superlative Old Masters. (p147)

Capitoline Museums Ancient sculpture is the main draw at the world's oldest public museums. (p32)

Museo Nazionale Romano: Palazzo Massimo alle Terme An overlooked gem boasting fabulous Roman sculpture and mosaics. (p82)

Museo Nazionale Romano: Palazzo Altemps Blazing baroque frescoes provide the background for classical sculpture. (p44)

Galleria Doria Pamphilj A lavish gallery full of major works by big-name artists. (p44)

Best Masterpieces

Sistine Chapel Home to Michelangelo's celebrated *Giudizio universale* (Last Judgment) and ceiling frescoes. (p135)

Pietà A work of sculptural genius and a highlight of St Peter's Basilica. (p139)

La Scuola di Atene The greatest of Raphael's frescoes in the Vatican Museums' Stanze di Raffaello. (p132)

Santa Teresa trafitta dall'amore di Dio The Chiesa di Santa Maria della Vittoria is home to this Bernini sculpture, one of the masterpieces of European baroque art. (p73; pictured left)

Ratto di Proserpina Another Bernini sculpture, this one depicting Pluto abducting Proserpina, at the Museo e Galleria Borghese. (p147)

Ragazzo col canestro di frutta Admire Caravaggio's technical mastery and fearless bravado in the Museo e Galleria Borghese. (p147)

Trionfo della divina provvidenza Head Palazzo Barberini for Pietro da Cortona's spectacular fresco. (p72)

Best Little-Known Gems

Museo Nazionale Etrusco di Villa Giulia Italy's premier Etruscan museum. (p147)

Castel Sant'Angelo Admire lavish Renaissance interiors in this brooding, landmark castle. (p142)

Mercati di Traiano Museo dei Fori Imperiali A museum set in Trajan's towering 2nd-century shopping mall. (p32)

Centrale Montemartini A former power station juxtaposes ancient sculpture with industrial machinery. (p107)

Best Modern Art

La Galleria Nazionale Study works by the giants of modern European art. (p148)

Museo Nazionale delle Arti del XXI Secolo Rome's premier contemporary arts museum. (p148)

Museo Carlo Bilotti Boasts a collection of metaphysical paintings by Giorgio de Chirico. (p148)

Best
Shopping

Rome enthralls with a fabulous portfolio of department stores, specialist shops, independent boutiques and artisan workshops – guaranteed to please the most hedonist of shoppers. 'Retro' is among the Roman shopping scene's many unique qualities, with jewel-like boutiques run by third-generation artisans, dusty picture-framing and basket-weaving workshops, historic department stores all oozing an impossibly chic, old-school glamour. Meander, explore backstreets, enjoy.

WJAREK/SHUTTERSTOCK ©

What to Buy

Rome is a top place to shop for designer clothes, shoes and leather goods. Foodie treats are another obvious choice and you'll find no end of delis, bakeries, *pasticcerie* (pastry shops) and chocolate shops. Homeware is another Italian speciality, and many shops focus on covetable kitchenware and sleek interior design.

Shopping Areas

For designer clothes head to Via dei Condotti (p64) and the area around Piazza di Spagna. You'll find vintage shops and fashion boutiques on Via del Governo Vecchio (p41) in the *centro storico*, and in the Monti district (p91). Testaccio (p113) is a good bet for foodie purchases, with one of Rome's best delis and a daily market.

Artisans

Rome has a surprising number of designers and artisans, who create and sell their goods in small, old-fashioned workshops. There are places where you can get a bag, wallet or belt made to your specifications, or order a tailored tie or dress.

☑ **Top Tips**

▶ Many city-centre shops close on Monday morning.

▶ Winter sales run from early January to mid-February, and summer sales from July to early September.

You'll find a number of these in the *centro storico*, Tridente and Monti areas.

Best Fashion

Re(f)use Ethical fashion: bags and jewellery made from upcycled objects by Rome-born designer Ilaria Venturini Fendi. (p64)

Tina Sondergaard Retro-inspired dresses, adjusted to fit, at this bijou Monti boutique. (p91)

Boutique shops on Via dei Condotti (p64)

Gente An emporium-style, multi-label boutique; essential stop for Roman fashionistas. (p64)

Manila Grace Essential homegrown label for dedicated followers of fashion. (p65)

Best Gourmet Food

Volpetti Bulging with delicious delicacies, and notably helpful staff. (p115)

Antica Caciara Trasteverina Wonderful, century-old deli in Trastevere brimming with gourmet cheeses and salami (can be vacuum-packed to transport home), dried foodstuffs etc. (p129)

Salumeria Roscioli Byword for foodie excellence, with mouthwatering Italian and foreign delicacies. (p52)

Biscottificio Innocenti Enchanting, old-world biscuit shop in a Trastevere backstreet. (p129)

Confetteria Moriondo & Gariglio A magical-seeming chocolate shop. (p51)

Best Bookshops

Almost Corner Bookshop Superbly stocked, English-language bookshop. (p129)

Feltrinelli International Limited but excellent range of latest releases in English, Spanish, French, German and Portuguese. (p91)

Best Markets

Porta Portese Rome's historic Sunday morning flea market on the banks of the Tiber. (p129)

Nuovo Mercato di Testaccio Enjoy colours and characters at Testaccio's neighbourhood market. (p113)

Campo de' Fiori One of Rome's best-known markets on a historic central piazza. (p51)

Best
Culture

The Romans have long been passionate about culture. Ever since crowds flocked to the Colosseum for gladiatorial games, the locals have enjoyed a good show, and cultural events draw knowledgeable and enthusiastic audiences. Rome has everything from opera to hip-hop, Shakespearean drama and avant-garde installations on the program: you're sure to find a style to suit.

Opera & Classical Music

Rome's abundance of beautiful settings makes it a wonderful place to catch a concert. Classical music performances – often free – are regularly held in churches, especially around Easter, Christmas and the New Year, while summer sees stages set up in outdoor locations across the city. Top venues, such as the Auditorium Parco della Musica, often host big-name Italian and international orchestras and performers.

Film, Drama & Exhibitions

Romans are great cinema-goers and although most films are dubbed you can still catch a movie in its original language (marked VO in listings – *versione originale*). Similarly, theatres tend to stage performances in Italian, but you might strike it lucky. You'll have no language problems enjoying the many art exhibitions that come to town.

Centri Sociali & Counterculture

Rome's alternative scene is focused on the city's *centri sociali* (social centres). These counterculture hubs, which started life as organised squats, gave rise to Italy's hip-hop and rap scenes in the 1980s and still stage alternative entertainment, be it

☑ **Top Tips**

▶ Tickets for concerts, live music and theatrical performances are widely available across the city.

▶ Hotels can often reserve tickets for guests, or you can contact the venue directly – check listings publications for booking details. Otherwise try **Vivaticket** (☏ 892 234; www.vivaticket.it) or **Orbis** (☏ 06 482 74 03; Piazza dell'Esquilino 37; ⏱ 9.30am-1pm & 4-7pm Mon-Sat; 🚇 Via Cavour).

poetry slams, indie fashion shows or drum-and-bass gigs.

Auditorium Parco della Musica (p148), designed by architect Renzo Piano

Best Classical Venues

Auditorium Parco della Musica Great acoustics, top international classical musicians and multiple concert halls. (p148)

Teatro dell'Opera di Roma Great, red-velvet and gilt interior for Rome's opera and dance companies. (p90)

Terme di Caracalla Wonderful outdoor setting for summer opera and ballet. (p111)

Best for Jazz

Alexanderplatz Rome's foremost jazz club, with a mix of international and local musicians. (p145)

Auditorium Parco della Musica Stages, among other things, the Roma Jazz Festival. (p148)

Charity Café Spindly tables and chairs, in an intimate space, hosting regular live gigs. (p90)

Big Mama An atmospheric Trastevere venue for jazz, blues, funk, soul and R&B. (p121)

Gregory's Jazz Club Popular with local musicians, a smooth venue close to the Spanish Steps. (p76)

Best for Live Music

Blackmarket Bar filled with vintage sofas and armchairs, great for

eclectic, mainly acoustic live music. (p90)

ConteStaccio Free live music on the Testaccio clubbing strip. (p115)

Lettere Caffè Live music plus poetry, comedy and DJs are on offer. (p128)

Best Theatres

Teatro Argentina Rome's premier theatre with a wide-ranging programme of plays, performances and concerts. (p51)

Teatro India The alternative home of the Teatro di Roma. (p51)

Best
For Kids

Despite a reputation as a highbrow cultural destination, Rome has a lot to offer kids. Child-specific sights might be thin on the ground but if you know where to go there's plenty to keep the little 'uns occupied and parents happy.

TRAVNIKOVSTUDIO/SHUTTERSTOCK ©

Best Museums

Explora – Museo dei Bambini di Roma (☎06 361 37 76; www.mdbr.it; Via Flaminia 80-86; adult/reduced €8/5; ☼entrance 10am, noon, 3pm & 5pm Tue-Sun; Ⓜ Flaminio) Near Piazza del Popolo is this hands-on museum for kids under 12, with interactive displays and a free play park.

Museo delle Cere (Wax Museum; ☎06 679 64 82; www.museodellecereroma. com; Piazza dei Santissimi Apostoli 67; adult/reduced €9/4.50; ☼9am-9pm summer, to 8pm winter; 🚍Via IV Novembre) Go face to face with popes, rock stars and footy players at Rome's cheesy wax museum.

Museo delle Mura (☎06 7047 5284; www. museodellemuraroma.it; Via di Porta San Sebastiano 18; admission free; ☼9am-2pm Tue-Sun; 🚍Porta San Sebastiano) Walk along a stretch of the Aurelian Wall at this small museum housed in one of Rome's ancient city gates.

Best Shopping

Bartolucci (Map p42, D3; www.bartolucci.com; Via dei Pastini 98; ☼10am-10.30pm; 🚍Via del Corso) A sure-fire kid pleaser, this toy shop will also charm parents with its wonderful wood-carved toys.

☑ Top Tips

▶ Cobbled streets make getting around with a pram or push-chair difficult.

▶ In a restaurant ask for a *mezza porzione* (child's portion) and *seggiolone* (high-chair).

▶ Buy baby formula and sterilising solutions at pharmacies. Disposable nappies (diapers; *pannolini*) are available from supermarkets and pharmacies.

▶ Under 10s travel free on all public transport in the city.

Best
Tours

Taking a guided tour is an excellent way of seeing a lot in a short time or investigating a sight in depth. In high season, book tours in advance.

Best Walking Tours

Roman Guy (https://the romanguy.it) Packages, led by English-speaking experts, include skip-the-line visits to the Vatican Museums (US$89), foodie tours of Trastevere and the Jewish Ghetto (US$84), and an evening bar-hop through the historic centre's cocktail bars (US$225).

A Friend in Rome (☑340 501 92 01; www. afriendinrome.it) Silvia Prosperi and her team offer a range of private tours covering the Vatican and main historic centre as well as areas outside the capital.

Best by Bus

Open Bus Cristiana (☑06 69 89 61; www. operaromanapellegrinaggi.

org; single tour €12, 24/48hr ticket €25/28) These hop-on hop-off bus tours are an easy means of getting around the main sights for families with young children and those who can't walk far.

Best by Bike or Scooter

Bici e Baci (☑06 481 40 64; www.bicibaci.com; Via Rosmini 26; bike tours from €30, Vespa tours from €145; ⏰8am-7pm Mon-Sat; ⓂTermini) Offers guided tours of the main historical sites by bicycle, Vespa, a Fiat 500 or funky three-wheeled Ape Calessino.

Vespa Style Roma (☑06 446 62 68; www. vespastyleroma.it; Via Milazzo 3a; Vespa rental per hour/day €15/69, e-bikes

PAOLI/PHOTOS/SHUTTERSTOCK ©

☑ Top Tip

▶ An advantage of taking a guided tour of big-ticket sights is that you can cut out the queue for tickets, skip the line to get in and occasionally gain access to parts of a building not usually open to the public.

per day €25; ⏰9am-7pm; ⓂTermini) Across the road from Stazione Termini; rents e-bikes and organises guided Vespa/e-bike tours (from €70/40).

Best **LGBTIQ**

The city has a thriving, if low-key, gay scene. There are relatively few queer-only venues but the Colosseum end of Via di San Giovanni in Laterano is a favourite hang-out and many clubs host regular gay and lesbian nights. There is also a popular gay beach, Settimo Cielo, outside Rome at Capocotta, accessible via bus 61 from Ostia Lido.

Attitudes

Rome is by nature a conservative city and its legislators have long looked to the Vatican for guidance on moral and social issues. That said, the city's gay community has taken steps out of the closet in recent times and while Rome is no San Fran on the Med and discretion is still wise, tolerance is widespread.

Events

Gay Village (www.gay village.it; Parco del Ninfeo, EUR; ⏰Jun–Sep; Ⓜ EUR Magliana) Rome's big annual LGBT event, held in EUR, attracts crowds of partygoers and an exuberant cast of DJs, musicians and entertain-ers. It serves up an eclec-tic mix of dance music, film screenings, cultural debates, and theatrical performances.

Venues

Coming Out (Map p100, B1; ☎06 700 98 71; www.comingout.it; Via di San Giovanni in Laterano 8; ⏰7.30am-2am; 🚇Via Labi-cana) On warm evenings, with lively crowds on the street and the Colos-seum as a backdrop, there are few finer places to sip a drink than this friendly gay bar.

L'Alibi (☎06 574 34 48; Via di Monte Testaccio 44; ⏰11.30pm-5am Fri & Sat; 🚇Via Galvani) A historic gay club, L'Alibi is still kicking, hosting regular weekend parties and

☑ Top Tips

▶ **Arcigay Roma** (☎06 6450 1102; www.arcigayroma.it; Via Nicola Zabaglia 14) is the Roman branch of Italy's national organisation for the LGBTIQ community.

▶ **Circolo Mario Mieli di Cultura Omosessuale** (☎06 541 39 85; www.mario mieli.org; Via Efeso 2a; ⏰9am-6pm Mon-Fri; Ⓜ Basilica San Paolo) organises debates, cultural events and social functions.

serving up a mixed mash of house, techno, hip-hop, Latino, pop and dance to a mixed gay and straight crowd.

Survival Guide

Survival Guide

Before You Go

When to Go

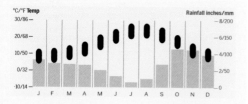

⇒ Winter (Dec–Feb)
Cold, short days. Museums are quiet and prices are low except at Christmas and New Year.

⇒ Spring (Mar–May)
Warm, sunny weather. Fervent Easter celebrations and azaleas on the Spanish Steps. Busy, with high prices.

⇒ Summer (Jun–Aug)
Very hot. Plenty of outdoor events. In August, Romans desert the city and hoteliers drop prices.

⇒ Autumn (Sep–Nov)
Still warm. Crowds die down and the Roma Europa festival is on. November brings rain and low-season prices.

Book Your Stay

⇒ Rome is expensive and busy; book ahead to secure the best deal.

⇒ Accommodation ranges from palatial five-star hotels to hostels, B&Bs, *pensioni* and private rooms. Hostels are the cheapest, with dorm beds and private rooms. B&Bs and hotels cover every style and price range.

⇒ Always try to book ahead, especially in high season (Easter to September) and during major religious festivals.

⇒ Ask for a *camera matrimoniale* for a room with a double bed; a *camera doppia* has twin beds.

⇒ When you check in you'll need to present your passport or ID card. Checkout is usually between 10am and noon. In hostels it's around 9am.

Useful Websites
Lonely Planet (www.lonely planet.com/italy/rome/hotels)

Author-reviewed accommodation options.

Cross Pollinate (www.cross-pollinate.com) Personally vetted rooms and apartments by the team behind Rome's super-efficient and stylish Beehive hostel.

Bed & Breakfast Association of Rome (www.b-b.rm.it) B&Bs and short-term apartment rentals.

Bed & Breakfast Italia (www.bbitalia.it) Rome's longest-established B&B network.

Rome As You Feel (www.romeasyoufeel.com) Apartment rentals; cheap studio flats to luxury apartments.

Best Budget

Generator Hostel (✆06 492 330; https://generator hostels.com; Via Principe Amedeo 257; dm €17-70, d €50-200; ❊ @ ☎; Ⓜ Vittorio Emanuele) Urban-chic (non)hostelling in Esquilino.

Althea Inn (✆06 9893 2666, 339 4353717; www. altheainn.com; Via dei Conciatori 9; d €120; ❊ ☎; Ⓜ Piramide) Designer comfort at budget prices.

Beehive (✆06 4470 4553; www.the-beehive.com; Via Marghera 8; dm €35-40, d without bathroom €80, s/d/tr €70/100/120; ⏱ reception 7am-11pm; ❊ ☎; Ⓜ Termini) Classy hostel near Termini.

Hotel Pensione Barrett (✆06 686 8481; www. pensionebarrett.com; Largo di Torre Argentina 47; s/d/tr €115/135/165; ❊ ☎; ▯ Largo di Torre Argentina) Welcoming old-school *pensione* with exuberant decor.

Best Midrange

Palm Gallery Hotel (✆06 6478 1859; www.palmgallery hotel.com; Via delle Alpi 15d; s €130-160, d €150-210; ❊ ☎ ❅; ▯ Via Nomentana, ▯ Viale Regina Margherita) Delightful hotel in elegant residential neighbourhood.

Arco del Lauro (✆06 9784 0350; www.arcodel lauro.it; Via Arco de' Tolomei 27; d €95-135, q €135-175; ❊ @ ☎; ▯ Viale di Trastevere, ▯ Viale di Trastevere) B&B bolthole in happening Trastevere.

Residenza Maritti (✆06 678 82 33; www.residenza maritti.com; Via Tor de' Conti 17; s/d/tr €120/170/190; ❊ ☎; Ⓜ Cavour) Hidden gem with captivating views over the Forums.

Nerva Boutique Hotel (✆06 678 18 35; www. hotelnerva.com; Via Tor de' Conti 3; d €143-300; ❊ ☎; Ⓜ Cavour) Stylish hideaway at the back of the Imperial Forums.

Best Top End

Villa Spalletti Trivelli (✆06 4890 7934; www.villa spalletti.it; Via Piacenza 4; d €625; ⓟ ❊ @ ☎; Ⓜ Spagna) Live like country-house nobility.

Hotel Campo de' Fiori (✆06 6880 6865; www. hotelcampodefiori.com; Via del Biscione 6; r €280-430, apt €230-350; ❊ @ ☎; ▯ Corso Vittorio Emanuele II) Classy four-star in the heart of the action.

Gigli d'Oro Suite (✆06 6839 2055; www.giglidoro suite.com; Via dei Gigli d'Oro 12; r €215-410; ❊ ☎; ▯ Corso del Rinascimento) Contemporary style in a 15th-century *palazzo* (mansion).

Fendi Private Suites (✆06 9779 8080; www. fendiprivatesuites.com; Via della Fontanella di Borghese 48, Palazzo Fendi; d from €900; ⓟ ❊ @ ☎; ▯ Via del Corso) Live the fashion-designer dream inside Palazzo Fendi.

Arriving in Rome

Leonardo da Vinci Airport (Fiumicino)

Rome's main international airport, **Leonardo da Vinci** (Fiumicino; ☎06 6 59 51; www.adr.it/fiumicino), is 30km west of the city. It's divided into four terminals: Terminals 1, 2 and 3 are for domestic and international flights; Terminal 5 is for American and Israeli airlines flying to the US and Israel.

The easiest way to get into town is by train, but there are also buses and private shuttle services.

Leonardo Express Train (one-way €14) Runs to/from Stazione Termini. Departures from Fiumicino airport every 30 minutes between 6.23am and 11.23pm; from Termini between 5.35am and 10.35pm. Journey time is 30 minutes.

FL1 Train (one-way €8) Connects to Trastevere, Ostiense and Tiburtina stations, but not Termini. Departures from Fiumicino airport every 15 minutes (half-hourly on Sundays and public holidays) between 5.57am and 10.42pm; from Tiburtina every 15 minutes between 5.01am and 7.31pm, then half-hourly to 10.01pm.

SIT Bus (Fiumicino) (☎06 591 68 26; www.sitbusshuttle.com; one-way/return €6/11) Regular departures from Rome Leonardo da Vinci (Fiumicino) Airport to Stazione Termini (Via Marsala) from 8.30am to 12.30am; from Termini between 5am and 8.30pm. All buses stop near the Vatican (Via Crescenzio 2) en route. Tickets are available on the bus. Journey time is approximately one hour.

Cotral Airport Bus (☎800 174471; www.cotralspa.it; one-way €5, purchased on the bus €7) Runs between Fiumicino and Stazione Tiburtina via Termini. Three to six daily departures including night services from the airport at 1.15am, 2.15am, 3.30am and 5am, and from Tiburtina at 12.30am, 1.15am, 2.30am and 3.45am. Journey time is one hour.

Ciampino Airport

Ciampino (☎06 6 59 51; www.adr.it/ciampino), 15km southeast of the city centre, is used by **Ryanair** (☎895 5895509; www.ryanair.com) for European and Italian destinations. It's not a big airport but there's a steady flow of traffic and at peak times it can get extremely busy.

To get into town, the best option is to take one of the dedicated bus services. You can also take a bus to Ciampino station and then pick up a train to Termini.

Airport Shuttle (☎06 420 13 469; www.airportshuttle.it) Transfers to/from your hotel for €25 for one person, then €6 for each additional passenger up to a maximum of eight.

SIT Bus – Ciampino (☎06 591 68 26; www.sitbusshuttle.com; to/from airport €6/5, return €9) Regular departures from the airport to Via Marsala outside Stazione Termini between 7.45am and 11.15pm; from Termini between 4.30am and 9.30pm. Get tickets on the bus. Journey time is 45 minutes.

Atral (www.atral-lazio.com) Runs regular buses between Ciampino Airport and Anagnina metro station (€1.20) and Ciampino train station (€1.20), where you can get a train to Termini (€1.50).

Stazione Termini & Bus Station

➡ Rome's main station and principal transport hub is **Stazione Termini** (www.romatermini. com; Piazza dei Cinquecento; Ⓜ Termini). It has regular connections to other European countries, all major Italian cities and many smaller towns.

➡ Train information is available from the Customer Service area on the main concourse to the left of the ticket desks. Alternatively, check www. trenitalia.com or phone ☏ 892 021.

➡ From Termini, you can connect with the metro or take a bus from Piazza dei Cinquecento out front. Taxis are outside the main entrance/exit.

➡ **Left luggage** (Stazione Termini; 1st 5hr €6, 6-12hr per hour €0.90, 13hr & over per

hour €0.40; 🕒 6am-11pm; Ⓜ Termini) is available by platform 24 on the Via Giolitti side of the station.

Getting Around

Public transport includes buses, trams, metro and a suburban train network. The main hub is Stazione Termini.

Metro

➡ Rome has two main metro lines, A (orange) and B (blue), which cross at Termini. A branch line, 'B1', serves the northern

suburbs, and line C runs through the southeastern outskirts, but you're unlikely to need those.

➡ Trains run between 5.30am and 11.30pm (to 1.30am on Fridays and Saturdays).

➡ All stations on line B have wheelchair access and lifts except Circo Massimo, Colosseo and Cavour. On line A, Cipro and Termini are equipped with lifts.

➡ Take line A for the Trevi Fountain (Ⓜ Barberini), Spanish Steps (Ⓜ Spagna) and St Peter's (Ⓜ Ottaviano–San Pietro).

➡ Take line B for the Colosseum (Ⓜ Colosseo).

Buses from Termini

From Piazza dei Cinquecento outside Stazione Termini buses run to all corners of the city.

DESTINATION	BUS NO
St Peter's Square	40/64
Piazza Venezia	40/64
Piazza Navona	40/64
Campo de' Fiori	40/64
Pantheon	40/64
Colosseum	75
Terme di Caracalla	714
Villa Borghese	910
Trastevere	H

Tickets & Passes

Public-transport tickets are valid on all of Rome's bus, tram and metro lines, except for routes to Fiumicino airport. They come in various forms:

BIT (*biglietto integrato a tempo,* a single ticket valid for 100 minutes; in that time it can be used on all forms of transport but only once on the metro) €1.50

Roma 24h (valid for 24 hours) €7

Roma 48h (valid for 48 hours) €12.50

Roma 72h (valid for 72 hours) €18

CIS (*carta integrata settimanale,* a weekly ticket) €24

Abbonamento mensile (monthly pass) Pass restricted to a single user €35; a pass that can be used by anyone €53

Roma Pass (valid within the city boundaries for two/three days €28/38.50)

Buy tickets at *tabacchi* (tobacconist's shops), at newsstands and from vending machines at main bus stops and metro stations. They must be purchased before you start your journey and validated in the machines on buses, at the entrance gates to the metro, or at train stations. Ticketless riders risk a fine of at least €50. Children under 10 years travel free.

Bus

➡ Rome's bus service is run by **ATAC** (📞06 5 70 03; www.atac.roma.it).

➡ The **main bus station** (Piazza dei Cinquecento) is in front of Stazione Termini on Piazza dei Cinquecento, where there's an **information booth** (Piazza dei Cinquecento; ⏱8am-8pm; Ⓜ Termini).

➡ Other important hubs are at Largo di Torre Argentina and Piazza Venezia.

➡ Buses generally run from about 5.30am until midnight, with limited services throughout the night.

➡ Rome's night bus service comprises more than 25 lines, many of which pass Termini and/or Piazza Venezia. Buses are marked with an 'n' before the number and bus stops have a blue owl symbol. Departures are usually every 15 to 30 minutes, but can be much slower.

Tram

Rome has a limited tram network. For route maps see www.atac.roma.it. The most useful lines include:

2 Piazzale Flaminio to/from Piazza Mancini.

3 Museo Nazionale Etrusco di Villa Giulia to/from San Lorenzo, San Giovanni and Trastevere.

8 Piazza Venezia to/from Trastevere.

19 Piazza del Risorgimento to/from Villa Borghese, San Lorenzo, Via Prenestina.

Taxi

➡ Official licensed taxis are white with an ID number and *Roma Capitale* on the sides.

→ Always go with the metered fare, never an arranged price (the set fares to and from the airports are exceptions).

→ Official rates are posted in taxis and at https://romamobilita.it/it/servizi/taxi/tariffe.

→ You can hail a taxi, but it's often easier to wait at a rank or phone for one. There are taxi ranks at the airports, Stazione Termini, main sights and piazzas.

→ The website www.060608.it has a list of taxi companies – click on the transport tab, then 'getting around' and 'by taxi'.

Essential Information

....

Business Hours

Banks 8.30am–1.30pm and 2.45–4.30pm Monday to Friday

Bars & cafes 7.30am–8pm, sometimes until 1am or 2am

Shops 9am–7.30pm or 10am–8pm Monday to Saturday, some 11am–7pm Sunday; smaller shops 9am–1pm and 3.30–7.30pm (or 4pm to 8pm) Monday to Saturday; some shops are closed Monday morning

Clubs 10pm–4am or 5am

Restaurants noon–3pm and 7.30–11pm (later in summer)

Electricity

230V/50Hz

230V/50Hz

Emergencies

Ambulance ☎118

Fire ☎115

Police ☎112, 113

Money

ATMS

→ ATMs (known in Italy as *bancomat*) are widely available in Rome and most will accept cards tied into the Visa, MasterCard, Cirrus and Maestro systems.

→ The daily limit for cash withdrawal is €250.

→ Always let your bank know when you are going abroad, in case it blocks your card when payments

Discount Cards

Archaeologia Card (adult/reduced €25/15; valid for 7 days) Entrance to the Colosseum, Palatino, Roman Forum, Museo Nazionale Romano (Palazzo Altemps, Palazzo Massimo alle Terme, Terme di Diocleziano, Crypta Balbi), Terme di Caracalla, Mausoleo di Cecilia Metella and Villa dei Quintili. Available at participating sites or by calling 📞06 3996 7700.

Omnia Card (€115; valid for 72 hours) Includes fast-track entry to the Vatican Museums and other major sites; audio guides for St. Peter's Basilica and Basilica di San Giovanni. Free travel on the Roma Cristiana Open Bus and unlimited public transport within Rome. Free entry to two sites, then 50% discount to extra sites. A 24-hour version is also available (€55). Details at www.omniakit.org.

Roma Pass (€38.50; valid for 72 hours) Includes free admission to two museums or sites, as well as reduced entry to extra sites, unlimited city transport, and discounted entry to other exhibitions and events. The 48-hour Roma Pass (€28) is a more limited version. Further information at www.romapass.it.

from unusual locations appear.

➡ Beware of transaction fees. Typically your home bank will charge a foreign exchange fee as well as a transaction fee. Check details with your bank.

Credit Cards

➡ Virtually all midrange and top-end hotels accept credit cards, as do most restaurants and large shops. Some cheaper *pensioni*, trattorias and pizzerias only accept cash. Don't rely on credit cards at museums or galleries.

➡ If your card is lost, stolen or swallowed by an ATM, telephone to have an immediate stop put on its use.

Tipping

Romans are not big tippers, but the following is a rough guide:

Bars Not necessary, although many people leave small change if drinking at the bar.

Hotels Tip porters about €5 at A-list hotels.

Restaurants Service (*servizio*) is generally included; if it's not, a euro or two is fine in pizzerias, no more than 10% in restaurants.

Taxis Optional, but most people round up to the nearest euro.

Public Holidays

Capodanno (New Year's Day) 1 January

Epifania (Epiphany) 6 January

Pasquetta (Easter Monday) March/April

Giorno della Liberazione (Liberation Day) 25 April

Festa del Lavoro (Labour Day) 1 May

Festa della Repubblica (Republic Day) 2 June

Festa dei Santi Pietro e Paolo (Feast of Sts Peter & Paul) 29 June

Ferragosto (Feast of the Assumption) 15 August

Festa di Ognisanti (All Saints' Day) 1 November

Festa dell'Immacolata Concezione (Feast of the Immaculate Conception) 8 December

Natale (Christmas Day) 25 December

Festa di Santo Stefano (Boxing Day) 26 December

Safe Travel

Rome is a safe city but petty theft can be a problem.

➡ Pickpockets are active in touristy areas such as the Colosseum, Piazza di Spagna and St Peter's Square.

➡ Be alert around Stazione Termini and on crowded public transport – the 64 Vatican bus is notorious.

➡ Never drape your bag over an empty chair at a streetside cafe or put it where you can't see it.

➡ Beware of gangs of kids demanding attention. If you notice that you've been targeted, either take evasive action or shout 'Va via!' ('Go away!').

➡ Always check your change to see you haven't been short-changed.

➡ In case of theft or loss, always report the incident to the police within 24 hours and ask for a statement.

Telephone Services

Local SIM cards can be used in European, Australian and unlocked US phones. Other phones must be set to roaming.

➡ Italian mobile phones operate on the GSM 900/1800 network,

which is compatible with the rest of Europe and Australia but not always with the North American GSM or CDMA systems – check with your service provider.

➡ The cheapest way of using your mobile is to buy a prepaid (*prepagato*) Italian SIM card. TIM (Telecom Italia Mobile; www.tim.it), Wind (www.wind.it), Vodafone (www.vodafone.it) and Tre (www.tre.it) all offer SIM cards and have retail outlets across town.

➡ Note that by Italian law all SIM cards must

Dos & Don'ts

Do...

➡ Greet people with a *buongiorno* (good morning) or *buonasera* (good evening).

➡ Dress the part – cover up when visiting churches and go smart when eating out.

➡ Eat pasta with a fork (not a spoon) and keep your hands on the table (not under it).

Don't...

➡ Feel you have to order everything on the menu. No one seriously expects you to eat a starter, pasta, second course and dessert.

➡ Order cappuccino after lunch or dinner. Well, OK, you can, but Romans don't.

➡ Wait for cars to stop at pedestrian crossings. You'll have to make the first move if you want to cross the road.

be registered in Italy, so make sure you have a passport or ID card with you when you buy one.

Toilets

Public toilets are not widespread but you'll find them at St Peter's Square and Stazione Termini (€1). If you're caught short, the best thing to do is to nip into a cafe or bar.

Tourist Information

Turismo Roma (www. turismoroma.it/?lang=en; 👫), Rome's official tourist website, has comprehensive information about sights, accommodation, city transport, as well as itineraries and up-to-date listings.

There are tourist information points at **Leonardo da Vinci (Fiumicino)** (International Arrivals, Terminal 3; ⏱8am-8.45pm) and **Ciampino** (Arrivals Hall; ⏱8.30am-6pm) airports, and locations across the city:

Piazza delle Cinque Lune (Map p42; Piazza delle Cinque Lune; ⏱9.30am-7pm; 🚌Corso del Rinascimento) Near Piazza Navona.

Stazione Termini (☎06 06 08; www.turismoroma. it; Via Giovanni Giolitti 34; ⏱9am-5pm; Ⓜ Termini) In the hall adjacent to platform 24.

Fori Imperiali (Map p30; Via dei Fori Imperiali; ⏱9.30am-7pm; 🚌Via dei Fori Imperiali)

Via Marco Minghetti (☎06 06 08; www.turismo roma.it; Via Marco Minghetti; ⏱9.30am-7pm; 🚌Via del Corso) Between Via del Corso and the Trevi fountain.

Via Nazionale (☎06 06 08; www.turismoroma.it; Via Nazionale 184; ⏱9.30am-7pm; 🚌Via Nazionale) In front of the Palazzo delle Esposizioni.

Castel Sant'Angelo (Piazza Pia; ⏱9.30am-7pm; 🚌Piazza Pia)

For information about the Vatican, contact the **Ufficio Pellegrini e Turisti** (Map p140; ☎06 6988 1662; St Peter's Square; ⏱8.30am-6.30pm Mon-Sat; 🚌Piazza del Risorgimento, Ⓜ Ottaviano-San Pietro).

Travellers with Disabilities

➡ Cobbled streets, paving stones, blocked

pavements and tiny lifts are difficult for the wheelchair-bound, while the relentless traffic can be disorienting for partially sighted travellers or those with hearing difficulties.

➡ All stations on metro line B have wheelchair access and lifts except for Circo Massimo, Colosseo and Cavour. On line A, Cipro and Termini are equipped with lifts.

➡ Bus 590 covers the same route as metro line A and is one of 19 bus and tram services with wheelchair access. Routes with disabled access are indicated on bus stops.

➡ If travelling by train, ring the national helpline ☎199 303060 to arrange assistance. At Stazione Termini, the **Sala Blu Assistenza Disabili** (☎800 90 60 60; Stazione Termini; ⏱6.45am-9.30pm; Ⓜ Termini) next to platform 1 can provide information on wheelchair-accessible trains and help with transport in the station. Contact the office 24 hours ahead if you know you're going to need assistance. There are similar offices at Tiburtina and Ostiense stations.

➡ Some taxis are equipped to carry passengers in wheelchairs; ask for a taxi for a *sedia a rotelle* (wheelchair).

➡ Download Lonely Planet's free Accessible Travel guide from http://lptravel.to/Accessible-Travel.

Visas

➡ Italy is one of the 26 European countries to make up the Schengen area.

➡ EU citizens do not need a visa to enter Italy – a valid ID card or passport is sufficient.

➡ Nationals of Australia, Canada, Israel, Japan, New Zealand, Switzerland and the USA do not need a visa for stays of up to 90 days.

➡ Nationals of other countries will need a Schengen tourist visa – to check requirements see www.schengenvisa info.com/tourist-schengen-visa/.

Language

Regional dialects are an important part of identity in many parts of Italy, but you'll have no trouble being understood in Rome or anywhere else in the country if you stick to standard Italian, which is what we've also used in this chapter.

The sounds used in spoken Italian can all be found in English. If you read our pronunciation guides as if they were English, you'll be understood. The stressed syllables are indicated with italics. Note that *ai* is pronounced as in 'aisle', *ay* as in 'say', *ow* as in 'how', *dz* as the 'ds' in 'lids', and that *r* is a strong and rolled sound.

To enhance your trip with a phrasebook, visit **lonelyplanet.com**. Lonely Planet iPhone phrasebooks are available through the Apple App store.

Basics

Hello.
Buongiorno.   bwon·*jor*·no

Goodbye.
Arrivederci.   a·ree·ve·*der*·chee

How are you?
Come sta?   *ko*·me sta

Fine. And you?
Bene. E Lei?   *be*·ne e lay

Please.
Per favore.   per fa·*vo*·re

Thank you.
Grazie.   *gra*·tsye

Excuse me.
Mi scusi.   mee *skoo*·zee

Sorry.
Mi dispiace.   mee dees·*pya*·che

Yes./No.
Sì./No.   see/no

I don't understand.
Non capisco.   non ka·*pee*·sko

Do you speak English?
Parla inglese?   *par*·la een·*gle*·ze

Eating & Drinking

I'd like ...   *Vorrei ...*   vo·*ray* ...

a coffee	*un caffè*	oon ka·*fe*
a table	*un tavolo*	oon *ta*·vo·lo
the menu	*il menù*	eel me·*noo*
two beers	*due birre*	*doo*·e *bee*·re

What would you recommend?
Cosa mi consiglia?   *ko*·za mee kon·*see*·lya

Enjoy the meal!
Buon appetito!   bwon a·pe·*tee*·to

That was delicious!
Era squisito!   *e*·ra skwee·*zee*·to

Cheers!
Salute!   sa·*loo*·te

Can you bring me the bill, please?
Mi porta il conto, per favore?   mee *por*·ta eel *kon*·to per fa·*vo*·re

Shopping

I'd like to buy ...
Vorrei comprare ...   vo·*ray* kom·*pra*·re ...

I'm just looking.
Sto solo guardando.   sto *so*·lo gwar·*dan*·do

How much is this?
Quanto costa   kwan·to kos·ta
questo?   kwe·sto

It's too expensive.
È troppo caro/   e tro·po ka·ro/
cara. (m/f)   ka·ra

Emergencies

Help!
Aiuto!   a·yoo·to

Call the police!
Chiami la   kya·mee la
polizia!   po·lee·tsee·a

Call a doctor!
Chiami un   kya·mee oon
medico!   me·dee·ko

I'm sick.
Mi sento male.   mee sen·to ma·le

I'm lost.
Mi sono perso/   mee so·no per·so/
persa. (m/f)   per·sa

Where are the toilets?
Dove sono i   do·ve so·no ee
gabinetti?   ga·bee·ne·tee

Time & Numbers

What time is it?
Che ora è?   ke o·ra e

It's (two) o'clock.
Sono le (due).   so·no le (doo·e)

morning	*mattina*	ma·tee·na
afternoon	*pomeriggio*	po·me·ree·jo
evening	*sera*	se·ra
yesterday	*ieri*	ye·ree
today	*oggi*	o·jee
tomorrow	*domani*	do·ma·nee

1	*uno*	oo·no
2	*due*	doo·e
3	*tre*	tre
4	*quattro*	kwa·tro
5	*cinque*	cheen·kwe
6	*sei*	say
7	*sette*	se·te
8	*otto*	o·to
9	*nove*	no·ve
10	*dieci*	dye·chee
100	*cento*	chen·to
1000	*mille*	mee·le

Transport & Directions

Where's ...?
Dov'è ...?   do·ve ...

What's the address?
Qual'è   kwa·le
l'indirizzo?   leen·dee·ree·tso

Can you show me (on the map)?
Può mostrarmi   pwo mos·trar·mee
(sulla pianta)?   (soo·la pyan·ta)

At what time does the ... leave?
A che ora   a ke o·ra
parte ...?   par·te ...

Does it stop at ...?
Si ferma a ...?   see fer·ma a ...

How do I get there?
Come ci si   ko·me chee see
arriva?   a·ree·va

bus	*autobus*	ow·to·boos
ticket	*biglietto*	bee·lye·to
timetable	*orario*	o·ra·ryo
train	*il treno*	eel tre·no

Behind the Scenes

Send Us Your Feedback

We love to hear from travellers – your comments help make our books better. We read every word, and we guarantee that your feedback goes straight to the authors. Visit **lonelyplanet.com/contact** to submit your updates and suggestions.

Note: We may edit, reproduce and incorporate your comments in Lonely Planet products such as guidebooks, websites and digital products, so let us know if you don't want your comments reproduced or your name acknowledged. For a copy of our privacy policy visit lonelyplanet.com/privacy.

Our Readers

Many thanks to the travellers who used the last edition and wrote to us with helpful hints, useful advice and interesting anecdotes: Rod Berrieman, Pilar Cajade, Matthew Gabhann, Julie Little, Peter Somers and Kate Storey.

Acknowledgements

Cover photograph: Teatro di Marcello, Luigi Vaccarella/4Corners ©
Contents photograph: Roman Forum, tupungato/Getty ©

Duncan's Thanks

A big thank you to fellow Rome author Nicola Williams for her suggestions and great work, and to Anna Tyler at LP for all her support. For their tips and help with research, *grazie* to Silvia Prosperi and Vania di Cicco at Frascati. Also a shout-out to Richard McKenna for his entertaining lunch company. As always, a big, heartfelt hug to Lidia and the boys, Ben and Nick.

Nicola's Thanks

Grazie mille to those who shared their Roman love and insider knowledge: Linda Martinez, Daniela & Lorenza, Elyssa Bernard, Fiona Brewer, Sian Lloyd & Lorna Davidson, Gina Tringali & Eleonora Baldwin, passionate art historians Molly McIlWrath & Daisy de Plume. Finally, kudos to my highly-skilled, enthusiastic, trilingual, family-travel research team: Niko, Mischa & Kaya.

This Book

This 5th edition of Lonely Planet's *Pocket Rome* guidebook was researched and written by Duncan Garwood and Nicola Williams. The previous two editions were written by Duncan and Abigail Blasi. This guidebook was produced by the following:

Curator Kate Mathews

Destination Editor Anna Tyler

Product Editors Elizabeth Jones, Anne Mason

Senior Cartographer Anthony Phelan

Book Designer Virginia Moreno

Assisting Editors Katie Connolly, Victoria Harrison, Gabrielle Innes, Susan Paterson, Monique Perrin, Fionn Twomey

Cover Researcher Naomi Parker

Thanks to Martine Power, Kirsten Rawlings, Kathryn Rowan, Lyahna Spencer, Tony Wheeler, Amanda Williamson

Index

See also separate subindexes for:

🍴 Eating p190

🍷 Drinking p190

🎭 Entertainment p191

🛍 Shopping p191

Our Writers

Duncan Garwood

From facing fast bowlers in Barbados to sidestepping hungry pigs in Goa, Duncan's travels have thrown up many unique experiences. These days he largely dedicates himself to Italy, his adopted homeland where he's been living since 1997. From his base in the Castelli Romani hills outside Rome, he's clocked up endless kilometres exploring the country's well-known destinations and far-flung reaches, working on guides to Rome, Sardinia, Sicily, Piedmont, and Naples & the Amalfi Coast. Other LP titles include *Italy's Best Trips*, the *Food Lover's Guide to the World*, and *Pocket Bilbao & San Sebastian*. He also writes on Italy for newspapers, websites and magazines.

Nicola Williams

Border-hopping is a way of life for British writer, runner, foodie, art aficionado and mum-of-three Nicola Williams who has lived in a French village on the southern side of Lake Geneva for more than a decade. Nicola has authored more than 50 guidebooks on Paris, Provence, Rome, Tuscany, France, Italy and Switzerland for Lonely Planet and covers France as a destination expert for the *Telegraph*. She also writes for the *Independent*, *Guardian*, lonelyplanet.com, *Lonely Planet Magazine*, *French Magazine*, *Cool Camping France* and others. Catch her on the road on Twitter and Instagram at @tripalong

Published by Lonely Planet Global Limited
CRN 554153
5th edition – Jan 2018
ISBN 978 1 78657 258 5
© Lonely Planet 2018   Photographs © as indicated 2018
10 9 8 7 6 5 4 3 2 1
Printed in Malaysia